SHE throughout **HISTORY**

I. Royal Icons & World Leaders

"Series of collected articles about the most iconic women
throughout history"

Author

Lina Soliman

Dedication & Brief Introduction

As a matter of fact, I deeply wanted to have someone I can express my sincere gratitude to, but unfortunately, I'm a standalone individual. Certainly, I received distinguished support from my beloved family to follow my dream of becoming a writer; but if I have to address my appreciation in regards to this book, I'd choose the "World Wide Web" for the tremendous amount of information and records to bring this book to light. So, THANK YOU GOOGLE!

This might seem awkward, but I tended to lean on the Internet, not only out of the fact that the internet really has what is required, but also to see how the most commonly used resource is talking about "what I call them," the founders of civilization.... "WOMEN".

While I chose to live shoulder to shoulder with nature, and as far away as I can go from modern life and huge buildings, I found it quite difficult to reach out to legitimately solid physical resources to write this book. Consequently, the internet was my most faithful companion with endless digital articles wrote by trustworthy history writers.

As a sincere feminist, I've always believed in the genuine power of women. Thus, during my journey to direct this book, I found out undoubtedly that women are not only omnipotent, but also with a levelheaded and steadfast will to simply "CHANGE THE HISTORY"

Whether you're with or against their doings, their accomplishments were glorious enough to be engraved in history books!

Table of Contents

Queen Victoria (1837-1901) - Queen of the United Kingdom of Great Britain and Ireland 4

Catherine the Great (1729 – 1796) - Empress of Russia 14

Catherine de' Medici (1519-1589) - Italian-born Queen of France 21

Cleopatra (69 BC-30 BC) - Egyptian Pharaoh 31

Isabella of Castile (1451-1504) - Queen of Castile 42

Boudicca - Queen of Britain 49

Empress Dowager Cixi of China (1835-1908) 53

Theodora (497-548) - Empress of Byzantium...................................... 60

Diana, Princess of Wales (1961–1997)... 67

Margaret Thatcher (1925–2013) – The Iron Lady 75

Indira Gandhi (1917-1984) – 1st Female Indian Prime Minister 81

Sirimavo Bandaranaike (1916-2000) - Prime Minister of Sri Lanka........... 89

Queen Victoria (1837-1901) - Queen of the United Kingdom of Great Britain and Ireland

Victoria (Alexandrina Victoria; 24th May 1819 – 22nd January 1901) was Queen of the United Kingdom of Great Britain and Ireland from 20th June 1837 until her death. She adopted the additional title of Empress of India on 1st May 1876. Known as the Victorian era, her reign of 63 years and seven months was longer than that of any of her predecessors. It was a period of industrial, cultural, political, scientific, and military change within the United Kingdom, and was marked by a great expansion of the British Empire.

Victoria was the daughter of Prince Edward, Duke of Kent and Strathearn (the fourth son of King George III), and Princess Victoria of Saxe-Coburg-Saalfeld. After both the Duke and his father died in 1820, she was raised under close supervision by her mother and her comptroller, John Conroy. She inherited the throne aged 18 after her father's three elder brothers died without surviving legitimate issue.

Though a constitutional monarch, privately, Victoria attempted to influence government policy and ministerial appointments; publicly, she became a national icon who was identified with strict standards of personal morality.

Victoria married her cousin Prince Albert of Saxe-Coburg and Gotha in 1840. Their children married into royal and noble families across the continent, earning Victoria the sobriquet "the grandmother of Europe" and spreading haemophilia in European royalty.

Edward VII (born 1841), married Alexandra, daughter of Christian IX of Denmark. Alfred, Duke of Edinburgh and of Saxe-Coburg and Gotha (born 1844) married Marie of Russia. Arthur, Duke of Connaught (born 1850) married Louise Margaret of Prussia. Leopold, Duke of Albany (born 1853) married Helen of Waldeck-Pyrmont.

Victoria, Princess Royal (born 1840) married Friedrich III, German Emperor. Alice (born 1843) married Ludwig IV, Grand Duke of Hesse and by Rhine. Helena (born 1846) married Christian of Schleswig-Holstein. Louise (born 1848) married John Campbell, 9th Duke of Argyll. Beatrice (born 1857) married Henry of Battenberg.

Namesakes

Around the world, places and memorials are dedicated to her, especially in the Commonwealth nations. Places named after her include Africa's largest lake, Victoria Falls, the capitals of British Columbia (Victoria) and Saskatchewan (Regina), two Australian states (Victoria and Queensland), and the capital of the island nation of Seychelles.

The Victoria Cross was introduced in 1856 to reward acts of valour during the Crimean War, and it remains the highest British, Canadian, Australian, and New Zealand award for bravery. Victoria Day is a Canadian statutory holiday and a local public holiday in parts of Scotland celebrated on the last Monday before or on 24 May (Queen Victoria's birthday).

At birth, Victoria was fifth in the line of succession after the four eldest sons of George III: the Prince Regent (later George IV); Frederick, Duke of York; William, Duke of Clarence (later William IV); and Victoria's father, Edward, Duke of Kent. The Prince Regent had no surviving children, and the Duke of York had no children; further, both were estranged from their wives, who were both past child-bearing age, so the two eldest brothers were unlikely to have any further legitimate children. William and Edward married on the same day in 1818, but both of William's legitimate daughters died as infants. The first of these was Princess Charlotte, who was born and died on 27th March 1819, two months before Victoria was born. Victoria's father died in January 1820, when Victoria was less than a year old. A week later her grandfather died and was succeeded by his eldest son as George IV. Victoria was then third in line to the throne after Frederick and William. William's second daughter, Princess Elizabeth of Clarence, lived for twelve weeks from 10th December 1820 to 4th March 1821, and for that period Victoria was fourth in line.

The Duke of York died in 1827, followed by George IV in 1830; the throne passed to their next surviving brother, William, and Victoria became heir presumptive. The Regency Act 1830 made special provision for Victoria's mother to act as regent in case William died while Victoria was still a minor. King William distrusted the Duchess's capacity to be regent, and in 1836 he declared in her presence that he wanted to live until Victoria's 18th birthday, so that a regency could be avoided.

Meeting with Prince Albert of Saxe-Coburg and Gotha

By 1836, Victoria's maternal uncle Leopold, who had been King of the Belgians since 1831, hoped to marry her to Prince Albert, the son of his brother Ernest I, Duke of Saxe-Coburg and Gotha. Leopold arranged for Victoria's mother to invite her Coburg relatives to visit her in May 1836, with the purpose of introducing Victoria to Albert. William IV, however, disapproved of any match with the Coburgs, and instead favoured the suit of Prince Alexander of the Netherlands, second son of the Prince of Orange. Victoria was aware of the various matrimonial plans and critically appraised a parade of eligible princes. According to her diary, she enjoyed Albert's company from the beginning. After the visit she wrote, "(Albert) is extremely handsome; his hair is about the same colour as mine; his eyes are large and blue, and he has a beautiful nose and a very sweet mouth with fine teeth; but the charm of his countenance is his expression, which is most delightful". Alexander, on the other hand, she described as "very plain".

Victoria wrote to King Leopold, whom she considered her "best and kindest adviser", to thank him "for the prospect of great happiness you have contributed to give me, in the person of dear Albert ... He possesses every quality that could be desired to render me perfectly happy. He is so sensible, so kind, and so good, and so amiable too. He has besides the most pleasing and delightful exterior and appearance you can possibly see". However at 17, Victoria, though interested in Albert, was not yet ready to marry. The parties did not undertake a formal engagement, but assumed that the match would take place in due time.

Early Reign

Victoria turned 18 on 24th May 1837, and a regency was avoided. Less than a month later, on 20th June 1837, William IV died at the age of 71, and Victoria became Queen of the United Kingdom. In her diary she wrote, "I was awoke at 6 o'clock by Mamma, who told me the Archbishop of Canterbury and Lord Conyngham were here and wished to see me. I got out of bed and went into my sitting-room (only in my dressing gown) and alone, and saw them. Lord Conyngham then acquainted me that my poor Uncle, the King, was no more, and had expired at 12 minutes past 2 this morning, and consequently that I am Queen".

Marriage

Albert and Victoria felt mutual affection and the Queen proposed to him on 15th October 1839, just five days after he had arrived at Windsor. They were married on 10th February 1840, in the Chapel Royal of St James's Palace, London. Victoria was love-struck. She spent the evening after their wedding lying down with a headache, but wrote ecstatically in her diary:

"I NEVER, NEVER spent such an evening!!! MY DEAREST DEAREST DEAR Albert ... his excessive love & affection gave me feelings of heavenly love & happiness I never could have hoped to have felt before! He clasped me in his arms, & we kissed each other again & again! His beauty, his sweetness & gentleness – really how can I ever be thankful enough to have such a Husband! ... to be called by names of tenderness, I have never yet heard used to me before – was bliss beyond belief! Oh! This was the happiest day of my life!"

Albert became an important political adviser as well as the Queen's companion, replacing Melbourne as the dominant influential figure in the first half of her life.

1842–1860

In 1845, Ireland was hit by a potato blight. In the next four years, over a million Irish people died and another million emigrated in what became known as the Great Famine. In Ireland, Victoria was labelled "The Famine Queen". In January 1847 she personally donated £2,000 (equivalent to between £178,000 and £6.5 million in 2016) to the British Relief Association, more than any other individual famine relief donor, and also supported the Maynooth Grant to a Roman Catholic seminary in Ireland, despite Protestant opposition.

Internationally, Victoria took a keen interest in the improvement of relations between France and Britain. She made and hosted several visits between the British royal family and the House of Orleans, who were related by marriage through the Coburgs. In 1843 and 1845, she and Albert stayed with King Louis Philippe I at château d'Eu in Normandy; she was the first British or English monarch to visit a French monarch since the meeting of Henry VIII of England and Francis I of France on the Field of the Cloth of Gold in 1520.

At the height of a revolutionary scare in the United Kingdom in April 1848, Victoria and her family left London for the greater safety of Osborne House, a private estate on the Isle of Wight that they had purchased in 1845 and redeveloped.

Demonstrations by Chartists and Irish nationalists failed to attract widespread support, and the scare died down without any major disturbances. Victoria's first visit to Ireland in 1849 was a public relations success, but it had no lasting impact or effect on the growth of Irish nationalism.

In early 1855, the government of Lord Aberdeen, who had replaced Derby, fell amidst recriminations over the poor management of British troops in the Crimean War. Victoria approached both Derby and Russell to form a ministry, but neither had sufficient support, and Victoria was forced to appoint Palmerston as prime minister.

On 14th January 1858, an Italian refugee from Britain called Felice Orsini attempted to assassinate Napoleon III with a bomb made in England. Victoria and Albert attended the opening of a new basin at the French military port of Cherbourg on 5th August 1858, in an attempt by Napoleon III to reassure Britain that his military preparations were directed elsewhere.

In November 1861, Albert was made aware of gossip that his son Albert Edward, Prince of Wales, had slept with an actress in Ireland. Appalled, he travelled to Cambridge, where his son was studying, to confront him. By the beginning of December, Albert was very unwell. He was diagnosed with typhoid fever by William Jenner, and died on 14th December 1861. Victoria was devastated. She blamed her husband's death on worry over the Prince of Wales's philandering. He had been "killed by that dreadful business", she said.

She entered a state of mourning and wore black for the remainder of her life. She avoided public appearances and rarely set foot in London in the following years. Her seclusion earned her the nickname "Widow of Windsor". Her weight increased through comfort eating, which further reinforced her aversion to public appearances.

She was persuaded to open Parliament in person in 1866 and 1867, but she was widely criticised for living in seclusion and quite a strong republican movement developed.

In late November 1871, at the height of the republican movement, the Prince of Wales contracted typhoid fever, the disease that was believed to have killed his father, and Victoria was fearful her son would die. As the tenth anniversary of her husband's death approached, her son's condition grew no better, and Victoria's distress continued. To general rejoicing, he recovered. Mother and son attended a public parade through London and a grand service of thanksgiving in St Paul's Cathedral on 27th February 1872, and republican feeling subsided.

Empress of India

After the Indian Rebellion of 1857, the British East India Company, which had ruled much of India, was dissolved, and Britain's possessions and protectorates on the Indian subcontinent were formally incorporated into the British Empire.

In the 1874 general election, Disraeli was returned to power. He passed the Public Worship Regulation Act 1874, which removed Catholic rituals from the Anglican liturgy and which Victoria strongly supported. She preferred short, simple services, and personally considered herself more aligned with the presbyterian Church of Scotland than the episcopal Church of England. Disraeli also pushed the Royal Titles Act 1876 through Parliament, so that Victoria took the title "Empress of India" from 1st May 1876. The new title was proclaimed at the Delhi Durbar of 1st January 1877.

Foreign Policy

the Queen's influence during the middle years of her reign was generally used to support peace and reconciliation. In 1864, Victoria pressed her ministers not to intervene in the Prussia-Denmark war, and her letter to the German Emperor (whose son had married her daughter) in 1875 helped to avert a second Franco-German war.

Between April 1877 and February 1878, she threatened five times to abdicate while pressuring Disraeli to act against Russia during the Russo-Turkish War, but her threats had no impact on the events or their conclusion with the Congress of Berlin. Disraeli's expansionist foreign policy, which Victoria endorsed, led to conflicts such as the Anglo-Zulu War and the Second Anglo-Afghan War. "If we are to maintain our position as a first-rate Power", she wrote, "we must ... be Prepared for attacks and wars, somewhere or other, CONTINUALLY." Victoria saw the expansion of the British Empire as civilising and benign, protecting native peoples from more aggressive powers or cruel rulers: "It is not in our custom to annexe countries", she said, "unless we are obliged & forced to do so".

The Second Reform Act

In regards to the Second Reform Act of 1867; the introduction of the secret ballot in 1872, which made it impossible to pressurise voters by bribery or intimidation; and the Representation of the Peoples Act of 1884 - all householders and lodgers in accommodation worth at least £10 a year, and occupiers of land worth £10 a year, were entitled to vote.

After the Second Reform Act of 1867, and the growth of the two-party (Liberal and Conservative) system, the Queen's room for manoeuvre decreased. Her freedom to choose which individual should occupy the premiership was increasingly restricted.

Later Years

On 2nd March 1882, Roderick Maclean, a disgruntled poet apparently offended by Victoria's refusal to accept one of his poems, shot at the Queen as her carriage left Windsor railway station. Two schoolboys from Eton College struck him with their umbrellas, until he was hustled away by a policeman. Victoria was outraged when he was found not guilty by reason of insanity, but was so pleased by the many expressions of loyalty after the attack that she said it was "worth being shot at—to see how much one is loved".

On 17th March 1883, Victoria fell down some stairs at Windsor, which left her lame until July; she never fully recovered and was plagued with rheumatism thereafter.

Although conservative in some respects - like many at the time she opposed giving women the vote - on social issues, she tended to favour measures to improve the lot of the poor, such as the Royal Commission on housing. She also supported many charities involved in education, hospitals and other areas.

She became the symbol of the British Empire. Both the Golden (1887) and the Diamond (1897) Jubilees, held to celebrate the 50th and 60th anniversaries of the Queen's accession, were marked with great displays and public ceremonies. On both occasions, Colonial Conferences attended by the Prime Ministers of the self-governing colonies were held.

Despite her advanced age, Victoria continued her duties to the end - including an official visit to Dublin in 1900. The Boer War in South Africa overshadowed the end of her reign. As in the Crimean War nearly half a century earlier, Victoria reviewed her troops and visited hospitals; she remained undaunted by British reverses during the campaign: "We are not interested in the possibilities of defeat; they do not exist".

Death

Victoria died at Osborne House on the Isle of Wight, on 22nd January 1901 after a reign which lasted almost 64 years, then the longest in British history. Her son, Edward VII succeeded her.

She was buried at Windsor beside Prince Albert, in the Frogmore Royal Mausoleum, which she had built for their final resting place. Above the Mausoleum door are inscribed Victoria's words:

"Farewell best beloved, here at last I shall rest with thee, with thee in Christ I shall rise again"

Sources:

https://en.wikipedia.org/wiki/Queen_Victoria
https://www.royal.uk/queen-victoria

Catherine the Great (1729 – 1796) - Empress of Russia

Catherine II was Empress of Russia for more than 30 years and one of the country's most influential rulers.

Sophie Friederike Auguste von Anhalt-Zerbst was born on 2nd May 1729 in Stettin, then part of Prussia (now Szczecin in Poland), the daughter of a minor German prince. In 1745, after being received into the Russian Orthodox Church, and changing her name to Catherine, she married Grand Duke Peter, grandson of Peter the Great and heir to the Russian throne.

The marriage was unhappy, but the couple did produce one son, Paul. In 1762 Catherine's husband became Tsar Peter III but he was soon overthrown with Catherine being declared empress. Peter was then killed shortly afterwards and it is not known whether Catherine had a part in his death. She subsequently had a series of lovers whom she promoted to high office, the most famous and successful of whom was Grigori Potemkin.

Catherine's major influences on her adopted country were in expanding Russia's borders and continuing the process of Westernization begun by Peter the Great. During her reign she extended the Russian empire southwards and westwards, adding territories which included the Crimea, Belarus and Lithuania. Agreements with Prussia and Austria led to three partitions of

Poland, in 1772, 1793, and 1795, extending Russia's borders well into central Europe.

Catherine began as a political and social reformer but gradually grew more conservative as she got older. In 1767 she convened the Legislative Commission to codify Russia's laws and, in the process, modernized Russian life. She presented the commission with her Nakaz, (or 'Instruction'), a strikingly liberal document that presented the empress's vision of the ideal government. The commission produced no desired results and the outbreak of war against the Ottoman Empire in 1768 provided a good opportunity to disband it.

The Pugachev Rebellion of 1774-1775 gained huge support in Russia's western territories until it was extinguished by the Russian army. Catherine realized her heavy reliance on the nobility to control the country and instigated a series of reforms giving them greater control over their land and serfs. The 1785 "Charter to the Nobility" established them as a separate estate in Russian society and assured their privileges. Catherine therefore ignored any concern she may previously have had for the plight of the serfs, whose status and rights declined further.

Catherine's main interests were in education and culture. She read widely and corresponded with many of the prominent thinkers of the era, including Voltaire and Diderot. She was a patron of the arts, literature and education and acquired an art collection which now forms the basis of the Hermitage Museum.

Female Artists

Catherine's rule brought about something of a golden period for female artists. While it was Peter I (reign 1682-1725) that brought about reforms that gave women greater freedom to pursue education it was during the mid-18th century, the time that Catherine the Great rose to power, that female artists also rose in Russia.

"Brandishing their newly won literacy, Russian women writers and poets, followed closely by Russian women composers, set pen to paper, starting in the mid-1700s," wrote Anne Harley, a professor of music at Scripps College, in a paper published in 2015 in the "Journal of Singing."

These female artists tended to be from the aristocratic class but they followed the lead of Catherine II ("the great") and other women who held power in Russia in the 18th century. "These female aristocrats followed a new model of empowered and extremely cultured womanhood, modeled by four women who ruled the Russian empire for more than two-thirds of the 18th century: Catherine I, Anna, Elisabeth, and Catherine II," wrote Harley in her paper.

Among the most prolific Russian female artists was Princess Natalia Ivanovna Kurakina (lived 1768-1831) who wrote at least 45 songs. "Kurakina's songs were so popular that Breitkopf (Petersburg) published a collection of eight of her French romances in 1795," wrote Harley.

Power and Love

Catherine was also a successful military ruler; her troops conquered a great deal of new territory. She also allowed a system of serfdom to continue in Russia, something that would contribute to a full-fledged revolt led by a pretender to the throne.

Catherine had no claim whatsoever to the Russian throne, according to Isabel de Madariaga, a professor emeritus of Slavonic Studies at the University of London in the opening of her book "A Short History of Catherine the Great" (Yale University Press, 2002).

Madariaga wrote that Catherine's opportunity came when her husband ascended to the throne as Peter III at the end of 1761. The two of them hated each other, and he ruled ineptly. "Though not stupid, he was totally lacking in common sense, and he quickly set about alienating all the powerful parties at court," Madariaga wrote. He embarked on a seemingly pointless military campaign against Denmark, alienated the Orthodox clergy by attempting to take over church lands and even tried to marry his mistress.

"Most of his policies were so unpopular at court, so lacking in judgment, that several groups started plotting to dethrone him," wrote Madariaga. Catherine got the jump on the others through her romantic relationship with Grigory Orlov, an officer in the Russian Guards. With the support of local military units, Catherine was proclaimed Empress of Russia in July 1762 while her husband was away from St. Petersburg, the capital. Peter III was then arrested, forced to abdicate the throne and ultimately killed.

Orlov would be one of many lovers that Catherine would have in her life. She alluded to her habit of often switching lovers in a letter she wrote to Prince Grigory Potemkin, a military leader with whom she had an affair in 1774-1775.

"The trouble is that my heart is loath to remain even one hour without love. It is said that human vices are often concealed under the cloak of kindness, and it is possible that such a disposition of the heart is more of a vice than a virtue, but I ought not to write this to you, for you might stop loving me or refuse to go to the army fearing I should forget you…" (From the book "The Russian Chronicles," 1998, Quadrillion Publishing, edited by Joseph Ryan).

Expanding the Empire

Catherine started her reign with Russia already in a relatively favorable military position. Before her reign, Russia's military had defeated the forces of Frederick the Great, king of Prussia, in battles at Gross-Jägersdorf (in 1757) and Kunersdorf (1759), victories that left Russia in a powerful position in Eastern Europe, wrote Simon Dixon, a professor at University College London, in his book "Catherine the Great" (Profile Books, 2009). He noted that with the death of the Polish king, Augustus III, in 1763, she was able to put one of her lovers, Stanislaw Poniatowski, on the Polish throne.

Poniatowski and Catherine ended up getting more than they bargained for. Catherine insisted that he grant rights to Poland's Orthodox and Protestant worshipers, something that offended many Polish Catholics. This issue led to a rebellion, and in the end Russian troops were sent into Poland to support Poniatowski. The presence of these Russian troops raised concerns among neighboring states that Russia had ambitions on their own territories, wrote researcher Robert Massie in his book "Catherine the Great: Portrait of a Woman" (Random House, 2011).

Massie noted that the sultan of Turkey felt the most threatened, fearing that Russian troops in Poland would be able to pour into the Balkans, threatening Istanbul itself. After discussions with French diplomats, and an incident with Russian troops at the Turkish border in October 1768, Turkey declared war on Russia.

Frederick the Great felt that the war would amount to nothing, wrote Massie, noting that the Prussian king called it a contest between "the one-eyed and the blind." This was to be proven wrong, however, as Russian troops made rapid advances in 1769, following them up with pivotal victories over the Turkish army at the Battles of Larga and Kagul, both fought in the summer of 1770. Also, in 1770, a Russian naval squadron reached the eastern Mediterranean, inflicting a defeat on the Turkish fleet.

Catherine's engagements in Poland and against Turkey worked favorably for her, noted Massie. In 1772, Poland was partitioned between Russia, Austria and Prussia, with subsequent partitions occurring in 1793 and 1795. Additionally, in 1774, after Russian troops were in a position to threaten Istanbul, Turkey sued for peace, with Russia gaining territories on the Black Sea coast and the Sea of Azov area.

Although Catherine didn't go into battle personally, delegating that responsibility to those with military expertise, she had proven her military mettle, gaining a vast amount of new territory and influence for Russia.

Serfdom and Rebellion

While Catherine enjoyed great military success, internally her country had a precarious social structure. Much of the population lived as serfs, in essence a form of slave. Their living conditions were horrible; Massie noted that few of the serfs working in the mines, foundries and factories lived to middle age.

Although Catherine is said to have personally opposed the institution, she tolerated it. In 1767, her government even published a decree condemning serfs who protested about their conditions.

"And should it so happen that even after the publication of the present decree of Her Imperial Majesty any serfs and peasants should cease to give the proper obedience to their landlords ... and should make bold to submit unlawful petitions complaining of their landlords, and especially to petition Her Imperial Majesty personally, then both those who make the complaints and those who write up the petitions shall be punished by the knout (whip) and forthwith deported to Nerchinsk to penal servitude for life..." read part of it. (Translation by G. Vernadsky from "A Source Book for Russian History" volume two, New Haven: Yale University Press, 1972, through Fordham University website).

Catherine's treatment of the serfs would come back to haunt her in 1773, when a man named Yemelyan Pugachev claimed to be Peter III (Catherine's executed husband) and staged an insurrection. Much of his rhetoric focused on gaining support from serfs and others from Russia's lower classes.

"We release you from all the taxes and financial burdens formerly inflicted on the peasants and all the people by wicked nobility and by bribe-taking town judges ..." he decreed as he approached the town of Penza, offering the people land ownership. In the end, Pugachev was captured and executed, and the institution of serfdom continued on after Catherine's death (Source of translation: the book "The Russian Chronicles").

Death and Succession

Catherine died quietly in her bed on Nov 17th, 1796, at the age of 67 after suffering a stroke. After her death, her enemies spread gossip about her that has endured for centuries: that she had died while having sex with a horse. Others claimed that she died on the toilet. Neither rumor was true.

Catherine was succeeded by Paul I, who was supposedly her son with Peter III (Paul's true father may have been Sergei Saltykov, one of Catherine's lovers). In any event, Paul did not last long on the throne; he was assassinated in 1801.

While the institution of serfdom would gradually be abolished in Russia during the 19th century, the wide gap in wealth between the nobility and peasantry would continue on. These social problems came to a boiling point once again after Russia entered World War I in 1914. As Russia's military position worsened and social conditions deteriorated at home, the Russian royal house lost support, with Nicholas II being executed in 1918, effectively ending the Russian royal family. The resulting civil war would see the rise of the world's first communist state, one that would eventually become a global superpower.

Sources:

http://www.bbc.co.uk/history/historic_figures/catherine_the_great.shtml

https://www.livescience.com/42006-catherine-the-great.html

Catherine de' Medici (1519-1589) - Italian-born Queen of France

Catherine de' Medici (1519-1589) was a Machiavellian politician, wife of Henry II of France, and later regent for her three feeble sons at the twilight of the Valois dynasty, who authorized the killing of French Protestants in the notorious Massacre of St. Bartholomew's Day in 1572.

Catherine de' Medici was never able to rule France as its monarch because the Salic Law restricted the succession solely to men. But this Machiavellian—whose father was Machiavelli's patron—ruled it as regent for nearly 30 years, and did everything she could to strengthen the position of her three weak sons on its throne. She presided over, and was partly responsible for, many of the horrors of the French Wars of Religion in the 1560s and 1570s, of which the worst was the massacre of Protestants gathered in Paris to witness the marriage of her daughter Marguerite Valois to Duke Henry of Navarre in 1572. Her calculating policies yielded short-term victories, but when she died in 1589 her hopes for her family's long-term future lay in ruins.

Catherine was born in 1519, daughter of a powerful Italian prince from the Medici family. Her mother died within a few days from puerperal fever and her father succumbed to consumption a week later at the age of 27, leaving her an orphan after less than one month of life. Her father's relatives, among them popes Leo X and Clement VII, took over her care, and she grew up in the midst of the stormy Italian Wars in which they were central actors. When a German army of the Holy Roman Emperor Charles V sacked Rome in 1527, the citizens of Florence took advantage of this eclipse of Medici power to restore their republic, and took the eight-year-old Catherine hostage. Escaping from Rome and hiring a group of mercenaries to recapture Florence, her uncle Clement VII was able to rescue her from her refuge in a nunnery.

In pursuit of Pope Clement's dynastic ambitions, 14-year-old Catherine was married in 1533 to 14-year-old Henry, duke of Orleans, younger son of King Francis I of France. The elaborate ceremony at Marseilles Cathedral was conducted by the pope himself, but her childlessness for the first ten years of marriage made her unpopular in the French court. With the help, as she believed, of astrologers—she was patroness of the seer Nostradamus and a lifelong dabbler in necromancy, astronomy, and astrology—she overcame this early infertility and gave birth to ten children, beginning in 1543. Few of them were healthy, however, and she, enjoying an iron constitution and great powers of recovery, would outlive all but one, Henry III, who would follow her to the grave in a matter of months. The death of her husband's older brother in 1536 made Henry and Catherine heirs to the throne, but the circumstances of his death increased Catherine's unpopularity. One of her retinue, Count Sebastian Montecuculi, was suspected of poisoning him to promote the interests of Catherine and, possibly, of France's enemy Charles V.

Catherine's husband, now Henry II, had spent several childhood years as a hostage at the Spanish court in Madrid. On his return, at the age of 11, he had been cared for by Diane de Poitiers, who was 20 years his senior. Despite this age difference, they became lovers, and throughout most of Henry's reign, which began in 1547, Diane completely eclipsed Catherine in influence over the king, though her age and her lack of beauty made Henry's attraction and loyalty to her something of a mystery at court. Diane was even given responsibility for raising Catherine's children, and she and Henry arranged the betrothal of the oldest son, Francis, to Mary, Queen of Scots in 1548. But in 1557, Catherine's coolness in an emergency won her new respect from Henry. He had lost the battle of St. Quentin to Philip II of Spain; when Paris itself was jeopardized, Catherine made a patriotic speech to the Parlement, persuaded it to raise more troops and money to continue the fight, and put to rest the old suspicion that she was more an Italian schemer than a true queen of France.

At the time of Catherine's birth in 1519 the Reformation was beginning with Martin Luther's criticism of the Catholic Church. The challenge to Rome's religious hegemony (dominance) began in Germany but soon spread throughout Europe. The French lawyer and theologian John Calvin, living and writing in Geneva, Switzerland, was particularly inspiring to many French men and women, who saw in his version of Christianity a truer form of their faith than that offered by a politicized and often corrupt Catholic Church. In France, for example, appointments and promotions in the Catholic Church were all at the king's disposal; political cronyism rather than piety and administrative skill led to advancement. French Protestants were known as Huguenots, and the rapid growth of their numbers among the nobility and upper classes as well as among ordinary folk soon made them a politically significant force; the Huguenots held their first general French assembly in 1559.

This was an era in which monarchs assumed that the integrity of their kingdoms depended on the religious uniformity of their peoples; religious schism of the kind which beset France by mid-century was unprecedented. The Catholic monarchs of France and Spain made peace at Cateau-Cambrésis in 1559 partly because they were bankrupt but also so that they could unite their forces against Protestantism. The treaty was sealed by the marriage of Philip II of Spain to Elisabeth, the teenaged daughter of Catherine and King Henry. At the joust held to mark the wedding celebrations, however, King Henry was fatally injured by a lance wielded by a Calvinist nobleman, the

Comte de Montgomery. It shattered his helmet, pierced his eye, and entered his brain. Henry's death a few days later brought their oldest son, 16-year-old Francis II, to the throne.

France was full of demobilized soldiers, many of them unpaid for months. Tax burdens on the peasants were heavy, and Calvinist preachers with their message of an uncorrupted faith found a receptive audience. Huguenot noblemen took action almost at once, organizing a conspiracy to overthrow or at least dominate the court of Francis II, and winning the active support of England's new Protestant queen, Elizabeth I. Then, at the city of Amboise, their military uprising failed, and the royal army arrested the leaders. In the presence of Catherine, her children, and Mary, Queen of Scots, 57 of the Huguenot leaders were hanged or beheaded. This retribution did not end the religious-political conflicts besetting France, however; from this time forward, the Huguenot Navarre family and the Catholic Guises led rival religious and court factions. The death of 16-year-old Francis II the following year made Catherine regent for her second son Charles, who now became King Charles IX at the age of ten.

Herself a lifelong Catholic but always with a degree of religious cynicism, Catherine appears never to have understood the passion with which many of her contemporaries lived their religious lives. For her, religious differences seemed at first to be bargaining chips in court intrigues, which might be smoothed away by tactful diplomacy. She permitted Admiral Gaspard de Coligny, an influential Huguenot, to act as Charles's chief advisor for a while, provoking three powerful noblemen, the duke of Guise, the cardinal of Lorraine, and the constable of France, to sink their own differences and make a three-way alliance, a triumvirate, for the defense of Catholicism against Coligny.

Catherine's miscalculation of the Reformation's impact on France was evident at the Colloquy of Poissy, 1561, when she tried to conciliate the

Catholic faction, under the cardinal of Lorraine, with the Huguenots, under the reform theologian and friend of Calvin, Theodore Beza. Far from coming to an understanding with one another, the two parties hardened their differences. In the poisoned atmosphere of broken negotiation, open hostilities began, marking the first of a succession of religious wars. Interrupted by truces, but marked by fierce vendettas, the conflict raged for a decade.

Charles IX was an unstable character, and as he matured, he came to dislike his mother and her favorite, younger son Henry. Charles, says the lively historian Henri Nogueres:

"had the figure of a sickly adolescent, too thin for its size, hollow-chested and with drooping shoulder…. his sallow complexion and bilious eyes betrayed liver trouble; he had a bitter twist at the corners of his mouth and feverish eyes…. He hunted in order to kill, for he soon acquired a taste for blood, and almost every day he needed the bitter sensation, the uneasy satisfaction of seeing the pulsating entrails and the hounds on the quarry".

Catherine found it relatively easy to dominate Charles, despite his growing resentment, and in the face of constant warfare she also tried to carve some order out of the fiscal and administrative chaos of the kingdom, to strengthen it for her sons' reigns. She took Charles on a long royal journey through his kingdom. She incorporated in 1565 a meeting with her son-in-law, Philip II of Spain, to discuss the continuing religious crisis. Philip disliked her apparent willingness to play off Catholics and Protestants against one another; in his view, she should have been doing more to advance the Counter-Reformation. But he also knew that France's weakness was a strategic benefit for Spain. It made French intervention to aid troublesome Dutch rebels against Spain far less likely. When Philip's wife and Catherine's favorite daughter Elisabeth died in childbirth in 1568, Catherine hoped he might marry her younger daughter Marguerite, but Philip was determined to take his French connection no further. Another blow to Catherine's politicking came the same year when her daughter-in-law, Mary, Queen of Scots, was captured by her English enemies and imprisoned, leaving Scotland open to Protestant domination and effectively ending a Franco-Scottish Catholic encirclement of Elizabethan England.

Through much of the 1560s, the two religious factions were at war while Catherine and Charles tried to avoid falling too heavily into either camp. The religious warfare was complicated further by English incursions into France itself, ostensibly in alliance with the Huguenots, but largely in pursuit of traditional English designs on northern France. The war was also complicated by a blood feud among the major families, brought on when the Huguenot leader Admiral Gaspard de Coligny ordered the assassination of the duke of Guise in 1563. As the fighting continued, especially in the third religious war, from 1568 to 1570, Huguenot armies attacked convents and monasteries, torturing and massacring their inhabitants, while Catholic forces, equally merciless, slew the Huguenots of several districts indiscriminately.

After a decade of war, the Peace of St. Germain in 1570 reconciled the two sides temporarily and led to Admiral Coligny's return to court. Among the treaty's provisions was the specification that Catherine's daughter Marguerite should marry Henry of Navarre, the Huguenot leader, that the Huguenots should be given several strongholds throughout France, and that Coligny could resume his position as a royal councilor. Catherine hoped that, as a moderate Huguenot, he might act to mollify his fellow Huguenots while she played the same role among Catholics. But Coligny quickly and tactlessly reasserted himself at court, becoming a friend and confidante of King Charles IX but arousing suspicions among Catholic courtiers that he was planning another coup. When Coligny discovered that Charles and his mother were at odds, he miscalculated and chose the king's side rather than Catherine's, provoking her furious resentment.

The city of Paris had remained friendly to the ultra-Catholic Guise party throughout these years of war, and most Parisians resented the concessions to Huguenots made at the Treaty of St. Germain. The population was, accordingly, restless and angry when a large Huguenot assembly entered their city in the summer of 1572 to celebrate the wedding. Marguerite Valois, the bride, was herself a stormy personality and an inveterate intriguer. When Catherine had discovered earlier that Marguerite was having an affair with the duke of Guise, she and Charles IX had beaten her senseless. The motive for this marriage alliance was that Henry of Navarre, though a Huguenot, would have a strong claim to the French throne if neither Charles IX nor Catherine's younger son Henry had a living heir. A connection to the Valois family would strengthen Navarre's claim as well as Catherine's prospects of continued influence. Marguerite, still in love with Guise, resisted the planned marriage, says historian Hugh Williamson:

"she and Henry of Navarre had known each other during their growing up at least well enough to be aware that they had no glimmer of sexual attraction for each other and even domestic accommodation was imperilled by such differences as her liking for at least one bath a day and his aversion to more than one a year. Also, he always stank of garlic".

She refused to give up her Catholic faith for this marriage, which was in any case imperiled when Henry's mother Jeanne of Navarre died suddenly during the negotiations which preceded it. In the fevered atmosphere of the time, many Huguenots were ready to believe that Catherine de' Medici had poisoned Jeanne, although that seems unlikely.

Catherine decided to dispose of Gaspard de Coligny once and for all. She accepted an offer from the Guise party to assassinate him, hoping that the outcome would be revived power for her own party. The assassin shot Coligny but failed to kill him, and Charles IX rushed to his side, promising a full inquiry and retribution against the assassins. But under interrogation from

Catherine and his younger brother Henry, Charles finally accepted their claim that Coligny was manipulating him, that Coligny planned to overthrow the whole Catholic court, and that he and the other Huguenot leaders should now be finished off in a preemptive strike. According to his brother Henry's diary, Charles at last shouted; "Kill the Admiral if you wish; but you must also kill all the Huguenots, so that not one is left alive to reproach me. Kill them all!".

By careful prearrangement, church bells began to ring at two in the morning of August 24th, Saint Bartholomew's Day, 1572. The bells signaled Catholic troops to begin, and at once they moved to kill the injured Coligny and other Huguenot leaders. The attacks became indiscriminate; all sense of order broke down. As widespread looting and fighting broke out across Paris, over 2,000 men, women, and children (including many people uninvolved in political and religious controversy) were shot or hacked to death. Similar massacres followed in the provinces, as Catholics seized the initiative against their local Huguenot rivals. King Charles feared that he had unleashed a revolution, but Catherine, according to one onlooker, "looks a younger woman by ten years and gives the impression of one who has recovered from a serious illness or escaped a great danger." A fourth civil war at once began, but by a strange turn of circumstances, leadership of the Huguenot party now fell to Catherine's youngest and most unscrupulous son Francis, duke of Alençon. Placing himself at the head of the Protestant forces and dreaming of a crown, he declared that his older brother Henry, who had just been elected to the throne of Poland, was no longer available as heir of France.

Henry, this third son of Catherine, was less easily dominated and manipulated than Charles. He was homosexual and had had a long succession of lovers. His mother tried to "correct" this propensity by ordering a banquet at which the food was served by naked women, but she could not succeed. Henry had spent the 1560s garnering the laurels of a successful general in the wars against the Huguenots. His victories won him the envy of King Charles

IX; whose physical frailty forbade campaigning. Catherine tried to marry Henry to Elizabeth I of England, but the "Virgin Queen" tactfully declined the offer and was equally obdurate against the wooing of the pathetic fourth brother, Alençon, whom she called her "frog." The only woman to excite Henry's interest, and to whom he sent ardent love letters signed in his own blood, was already married to the prince of Conde. Henry did not relish the prospect of going to Poland, even though his mother's judicious distribution of bribes to the electors there had secured the throne for him, but at last he set out. His departure prompted another Huguenot uprising, in which Alençon, Henry of Navarre, and Marguerite Valois were all implicated as conspirators. With her usual energy, Catherine coordinated forces to quell it, and with her usual decisiveness, she witnessed the executions of the ringleaders Montgomery, La Mole, and Coconnas. She also witnessed the death of her son King Charles, aged 24. She now recalled her favorite, Henry, to his hereditary kingdom.

Henry III was crowned in 1575 and married in the same year to Louise of Lorraine, but they had no children to carry on the Valois line. From this time on, Catherine entrusted family fortunes more wholeheartedly to the Catholic Guise family, and approved the formation of the Catholic League in 1576 which marched to triumph against the Huguenots. Henry's homosexual favorites predominated at court. When the Guise provoked a duel and killed two of them, Quelus and Saint-Megrim, Henry conceived an implacable hatred against them. Another round of blood feuding began despite Catherine's continued urging that Henry must settle his differences with the Guise for the sake of national and Catholic security.

Catherine remained politically active until the end of her life, touring France on Henry's behalf and trying to assure the loyalty of its many fractured and war-torn provinces. She also amassed a huge collection of books and paintings, built or enlarged some of Paris's finest buildings, including the

Tuileries Palace, and carried on to the end her fascination with astrology. She was fat and gouty by 1589 and was taken ill that year from the exertion of dancing at the marriage of one of her granddaughters. She lived just long enough to hear that Henry's bodyguards had murdered Guise; this news, writes Williamson, "destroyed her will to live, for it epitomized her failure. Her idolized son, for whom she had spent her whole life, had destroyed all that she had built and rejected everything she had taught him." Later that year, Henry III in turn died, assassinated by a Dominican friar, Jacques Clement, who regarded him a traitor to the faith for joining Henry of Navarre against the Catholic League. In this way, the Valois dynasty came to an end. Ironically it was the Huguenot prince Henry of Navarre who succeeded to the throne, though he was unable to sit upon it until 1593 when he cynically adopted the Catholic faith with the famous remark, "Paris is worth a Mass".

Source:

https://www.encyclopedia.com/ **Full link:** https://rb.gy/tv7jde

Cleopatra (69 BC-30 BC) - Egyptian Pharaoh

Cleopatra VII is one of the most famous women who has ever lived. Her story has inspired poets, dramatists, and artists for more than 2,000 years. Through cunning and guile, she survived to rule Egypt as all of her siblings perished by the wayside. Her famed beauty and charm led to one of the most celebrated romances in history - and the Ancient world's ultimate tragedy. Let's get up close and personal with the original Queen of the Nile, Cleopatra.

The Early Years

By the time of the birth of Cleopatra VII in 69 BCE, Egypt had a 3000-year-old history of power and decline. The country was ruled by a dynasty of pharaohs, each with the name of Ptolemy, who had arrived from Macedonia in 323 BCE. Now, however, they faced the danger of invasion from the menacing Roman empire.

The first Ptolemies had ruled benevolently, but their descendants, including Cleopatra's father proved to be weak, even foolish leaders. As a result, Cleopatra's early years were unsettled. She knew that her family was at war – with the people it ruled, and with itself. The people suffered under the cruelty of Ptolemy XII, Cleopatra's father, and they resented his alliance with Rome.

When Cleopatra was just four years old, the citizens of Alexandria rioted and chased Ptolemy out of Egypt. He fled to Rome and Cleopatra's older sister Berenice became queen. Three years later Ptolemy returned to Egypt. With the help of Roman general Pompey, he snatched back power from Berenice and ruled again as Pharaoh. One of his first orders was for his oldest daughter to be executed.

Cleopatra now had two surviving sisters and two younger brothers. All of Ptolemy's children hoped to eventually rule, which made them rivals. Shortly after the execution of Berenice, the next oldest daughter of Ptolemy, Cleopatra Tryphana died in mysterious circumstances. Many historians believe that she was poisoned by one of her siblings.

Now Cleopatra had only one sister still alive – the youngest Arsinoe. She must have wondered how long she would survive. Her two younger brothers were both named Ptolemy according to the custom. They would both eventually become rulers of Egypt – as Ptolemy XIII and Ptolemy XIV.

By the time she was fourteen, Cleopatra was Ptolemy's oldest living daughter. When he died, she would become queen as the wife of her younger brother Ptolemy XIII. For the young girl, the prospect filled her with both excitement and terror. Vividly recalling the fate of her two sisters, she feared that enemies might try to also kill her. But the young girl was clever. She had made friends with powerful courtiers who she felt would protect her.

Cleopatra was groomed for rulership from her early teens. She learned new languages, including Egyptian, which surprisingly was not spoken in the royal court – all her family members spoke Greek. She also used religion to support her claim to the throne, claiming to be the daughter of the Sun-God, an ancient royal title.

Cleopatra and her husband-brother, with their father having died, began their reign. It was 51 BCE and she was nearly 18 years of age, 10 years older than the new king. This allowed her to assume full responsibility for ruling the country.

It was a particularly complex time. In addition to domestic problems, which included a discontented peasantry, brought to its knees by famine, not to mention the hostility of other members of her own family, there were problematic foreign relations. The most pressing issue was the unrelenting demand for taxes coming Rome. In spite of the requirement of having her husband, Ptolemy XIII, appointed to rule with her, she didn't take kindly to having him tagging along. Her solution was to oust him from his position and rule alone for the next eighteen months.

Sibling Rivalry

One thing that Cleopatra knew was that she could not beat the Romans at their military game at this point, so she had to take off where her father had left off and keep appeasing the Roman overlords. She attempted damage control by working with the Roman oppressors in the hope that they would give up Egypt entirely.

Like her father she chose survival, but she had one advantage over him – Cleopatra was quite clever, and she knew how to play the cards she was dealt to her best advantage. She would continue to do so throughout her reign, up until the very end. She wasn't about to fold her hand if she could see any way to play to the best of her ability, and she would bluff if necessary. She would eliminate every other foe in the game and keep a few aces up her sleeve by winning key Alexandrians, Romans and the priests over to her side. She was a brilliant strategist, even at the young age at which she became co-regent.

Of course, given that she was ruling Egypt, and given the tempestuous history of her family, nothing was going to come that easy to a new ruler, especially a female one. Her little brother had his supporters, or should I say, his controllers, and they wanted to have the power in their hands, not

Cleopatra's. When I say 'they', I am speaking mainly of a man named Gnaeus Pompey, who at the time was the supreme controller of Rome, the man who gave her father the title king, and the person to whom was given the right to possess Cyprus. It is highly likely that Pompey saw Cleopatra as too smart to be simply mollified as her father had been. She would be hard to control and a constant threat to Roman dominance over Egypt. Her little brother needed some assistance and this was given in the form of Roman support: Pompey would show up occasionally to formally recognize the little brother over the big sister as ruler of Egypt.

With Pompey's backing, Ptolemy XIII went to war with his big sister, driving her from power. In 49 CE, Cleopatra discovered that her husband was plotting with Pompey to send soldiers to kidnap and possibly kill her. She knew that she must leave Egypt and so set sail for Syria. There she hoped to recruit an army to help her win back the throne from her now sixteen-year-old husband/brother.

Cleopatra chose to flee to Syria because the Ptolemies had once ruled there. The king of Syria was also an enemy of Rome. Like Cleopatra, he feared that his own country would be taken over by the mighty Roman empire. She took her only surviving sister, Arsinoe, into exile with her. This was partly to protect the younger girl from her brother's wrath, but also to stop her from seizing the throne for herself.

Enter Julius Caesar

While these dramas were playing out in the Ptolemaic dynasty, up north a bloody civil war was taking place. General Julius Caesar battled and defeated the forces of General Pompey. Pompey arrived in Pellucidum, Egypt hoping to get money, food, men and ships because he was running low on what he needed to defeat Caesar. Up until that time the Egyptians had been on the receiving end of much support from Rome due to the relationship established between Cleopatra's father and Pompey before Caesar rose up to challenge the Roman general. And now that Pompey had just lost badly to Caesar in Pharsalus, he needed Egypt's help.

Meanwhile Caesar was in pursuit and also looking for aid for his military needs. He arrived in Alexandria with a rather modest military force. However, it seemed to the young Egyptian king and his advisers that Caesar was going to be eventual victor in Rome. If the king continued to support Pompey to continue his war against Caesar on Egyptian soil, the battles could devastate Egypt. And, if Pompey eventually lost, Caesar would be enraged against the Egyptian rulership.

Caught between a rock and a hard place, as soon as Pompey landed with his troops at Pelessium, Ptolemy XIII had Pompey ambushed and killed. He then delivered Pompey's head to Caesar. However, the king miscalculated how happy Caesar would be to see his enemy's head presented to him by the Egyptian king. Pompey may have been his rival, but it was up to Caesar to decide Pompey's fate, not have the upstart Egyptian king usurp the right.

Even though he was horrified by the brutal murder of Pompey, Caesar wanted to keep the peace – he had come to Egypt to collect a huge sum of money that he claimed Cleopatra's father had owed him. He ordered both Ptolemy and Cleopatra to meet with him to discuss a peace treaty.

The now twenty-one-year-old queen saw her opportunity to act. She slipped past Ptolemy's general Achillas, who was blocking Pellucidum, and sailed along the coastline to Alexandria by way of the Nile. Then she went to see Caesar at the palace. Cleopatra had developed into a very mature and savvy young woman. Legend tells us that she secreted her in a rolled-up bedroll in order to get into the palace, but this has largely been debunked. She did not need to go to quite so covert lengths to get an audience with Caesar in Alexandria. She had been communicating with him from her post over the border. Surely, before sneaking past Achillas, and heading toward Alexandria, she had sent word to Caesar that she was coming or he had sent word to her telling her to come; either way, it likely was no surprise that Cleopatra was arriving in the harbor that night.

Apparently, Cleopatra donned her most impressive outfit and took great effort to look her most beautiful for her audience with Caesar. Whatever she did, it worked a treat and Caesar ordered that she be restored to her throne.

Naturally, when Ptolemy arrived to find Cleopatra in the palace reinstalled as co-regent he was not at all pleased. In fact, he threw a right royal fit. As impressed as Caesar was with the queen, he wisely took into consideration the support that her brother had among many of the upper crust Alexandrians, and so handled the situation quite astutely. He wisely read to brother and sister the will of their father, which stated that he wanted them to rule together.

But the young king was not appeased. He ran out of the palace and threw down his crown in a terrible rage. An amused Caesar allowed Ptolemy to leave the city and join his sister, Arsinoe, in Sicily. Days after the Alexandrian war ended, the abdicated king's body was found lying in the harbor.

Seducing Caesar

For the first time in years, Cleopatra now felt safe. Her enemy husband, along with his advisors, were dead and Caesar had promised to protect her and her new husband – her surviving 11-year-old brother, Ptolemy XIV. With Caesar, she sailed down the Nile in order to meet her subjects and impress them with her power. Rumors spread that she was pregnant with Caesars' child which came to be named Caesarion. When Caesar returned to Rome, he left 15,000 of his finest soldiers to guard the queen.

After taking control of Egypt, Cesar returned to Rome, where he was hailed as a hero. Before long, Cleopatra had come north to join him. She claimed that the trip was to negotiate a peace treaty between Egypt and Rome, but she also wanted to make sure of Caesar's protection. She did not want her younger brother or his advisers to try to seize power in Egypt while she was away.

Many Romans chafed the relationship between Cleopatra and Caesar. It was widely feared that Caesar would name Caesarion as his heir and that Cleopatra would then have a hold on the Roman Empire through her son.

Caesar celebrated his victories by parading his captives through the streets of Rome. Cleopatra's sister Arsinoe, who had led the Egyptian army against Caesar, was dragged through the streets bare headed and in chains. It was a disgrace for a woman to appear in public this way – it was the custom for Egyptian women to wear a long cloak and veil outside of their homes. However, Arsinoe was lucky – unlike other prisoners she was not killed. Caesar felt that the Romans might riot if they saw a princess publicly executed.

To give thanks for the victory at the battle of Pharsalus, Caesar built a new temple in Rome. He also paid for a beautiful statue of Cleopatra to be put on display in the temple – it showed her as a mother holding Ceasarion in her arms.

Crisis

As a reward for his victories, the Senate made Caesar dictator for life. But some Romans feared that Caesar was becoming too powerful and that he wanted to be king. About sixty conspirators decided that Caesar had to be killed. The plot, which was led by Brutus and Cassius, was carried through immediately following a Senate meeting in 44 BCE.

The shocking news of Caesar's murder spread through the Roman empire like wildfire. Cleopatra – who was in Rome at the time of the assassination – lost no time in hurrying back to Egypt. Now that Caesar, her protector, was dead, her kingdom was once more in danger.

Many hostile nations saw Egypt as a rich prize and hoped to conquer it. Cleopatra kept her son, Caesarion close by her side, because she feared that he might be murdered by Caesar's enemies.

On her return to Egypt, Cleopatra found that her sister Arsinoe, who had been released from roman captivity, was plotting with an anti-Caesar faction in the hope of seizing power. Many of the nobles in the Egyptian court supported Arsinoe and joined her in her conspiracy against Cleopatra.

At this time, the nation was suffering a crisis due to failure of Nile floods. There was not enough water in the river to spread rich mud over the fields to irrigate them. As a result, farmers crops and animals died, and many families suffered from famine and disease. Many nobles and officials were angry that Cleopatra did not take moves to help the famine victims. The tenuous situation for Cleopatra required a new Roman protector who she could lean on. It came in the form of Mark Antony.

Caesar's murder led to three terrible tears of warfare in Rome, as different groups of Roman senators and members of leading Roman families struggled to take control. The rival armies were led by three powerful men, and each hoped to take Caesar's place as ruler. Their names were Octavian (who was Caesar's nephew), Mark Antony and Marcus Lepidas. Finally, in 42 BCE, the Roman lands were divided among the three. Antony took control of the entire eastern Mediterranean region, which included Egypt.

The Great Seduction

Though he had control of Egypt, Antony still needed Cleopatra's support, and he feared that she might support his enemies. He needed gold from Egypt in order to pay his armies to keep control of his share of the empire, along with Egypt's grain in order to feed his men. Antony wrote to Cleopatra and when she did not reply, he summoned her to meet him.

Cleopatra was in no hurry to respond to Antony. Instead, she deliberately took her time. She knew that Antony needed Egypt's gold and in return she planned to ask for his protection. She also wanted his help to kill her enemies – including her sister Arsinoe.

As Antony waited for Cleopatra to arrive to the planned meeting in Tarsus, he heard news of large crowds gathering to witness an amazing sight. Cleopatra was sailing up the River Cydnus in a barge with a gilded poop, its sails spread purple, is rowers urging it in with silver oars to the sound of the flute blended with pipes and lute. The sails were made of silk, a rare and costly cloth from China. It was a floating palace.

The queen herself was dressed as the Greek Goddess of Love, Aphrodite. She lay on a couch beneath a canopy of gold cloth. Mark Antony was mesmerized and he invited Cleopatra to dine with him. But the queen refused, insisting that he join her on her royal barge. She took great care with her preparations – she wanted Antony to be delighted, astonished and, most importantly, impressed. She arranged for her barge to be decorated with thousands of tiny oil lamps and glittering, flickering patterns of lights.

Cleopatra met Antony several times during her visit to Tarsus. On each occasion she dressed as the Goddess Aphrodite. She offered Antony crowns of vine leaves, a symbol of Dionysus, the Greek God of wine. She was reminding Antony that, according to legend, Tarsus was the place where Aphrodite and Dionysus met and fell in love.

Cleopatra's seduction worked. Her dramatic visit to Tarsus had won Antony's support in her struggle to remain ruler of Egypt. Antony forgot his war against the Parthians and hurried to Egypt. They spent the winter of 41 BCE in Alexandria together, during which time Cleopatra hardly left Antony's side. During this time, her two remaining siblings, Arsinoe and Ptolemy XIV were put to death. Shortly thereafter, Cleopatra became pregnant.

Antony did not remain in Egypt to see the birth of his twins – a boy and a girl. In 40 BCE he had to return to Rome because his wife, Fulva, was leading a rebellion against Octavian.

Cleopatra continued to rule Egypt, but Antony did not return for another four years. When he sailed back in 36 BCE, after a disastrous defeat in Parthia, Cleopatra welcomed him. She needed a strong ally to help her keep Egypt independent.

Antony planned to set up an empire in North Africa and the Middle east to challenge his rivals in Rome. Cleopatra supported his plans because they would increase her own power. In 35 BCE, the pair had a third child, a son who they named Ptolemy Philadelphus. Early in 34, Antony invaded Armenia, returning to Alexandria in triumph. In a magnificent celebration Cleopatra was crowned 'Queen of the Kings'.

The couple's young children were given royal titles over Middle Eastern lands.

A Tragic End

Top Roman politicians, led by Caesar's nephew Octavian, were shocked by reports of Antony and Cleopatra's bid to set up an empire of their own. They were also angry that Antony had divorced his Roman wife. An outraged Octavian personally declared war against Cleopatra – and all of Egypt.

Even though Antony had tried to avoid conflict with Rome, it had now become impossible to avoid. This was especially so after the Roman Senate found out about his will, in which he declared his intention to be buried in Egypt beside Cleopatra. Antony was dismissed from all public appointments. Even though the army assembled by Antony and Cleopatra was larger, the famous battle of Actium in September of 31 BCE constituted a first fundamental step toward their defeat.

By now they were both considered foreigners and enemies of Rome. Antony succeeded in taking Pelusium and getting close to the gates of Alexandria in the spring of 30 BCE. A mad whirl of events followed; rumor had it that Cleopatra – shut in the mausoleum that she had built for herself – was dead. On hearing this news, denied immediately after, but too late, Antony wounded himself fatally and as he was dying was taken to the mausoleum. Cleopatra wept for Antony and tried in various ways to take her own life but she was watched over by Octavian's men who wanted to take her back to Rome, alive and in chains, as a symbol of the great Roman triumph over the enemy from the East. A few days before her departure, however, Cleopatra managed to evade surveillance and killed herself, probably with snake poison brought into the prison in a basket.

Cleopatra was the last independent ruler of Egypt, and her death marked the end of over 3,000 glorious years of Egyptian civilization and Egyptian power. Yet, she could not bear to live while foreigners ruled her beloved country. At her death, Egypt lost its most famous – and possibly its greatest – queen.

Source:

https://biographics.org/cleopatra-biography-queen-of-egypt/

Isabella of Castile (1451-1504) - Queen of Castile

Bold, strategic, and steady, Isabella of Castile navigated an unlikely rise to the throne and ushered in a golden age for Spain.

ISABELLA OF CASTILE should never have been queen. Born on April 22nd, 1451, she was the second child of King John II of Castile. The king already had an heir, Henry, a 26-year-old son from his first marriage, making him Isabella's half-brother. The king's second wife, Isabella of Portugal, would deliver a son, Alfonso, two years later, making Isabella third in line.

Her sex and her birth order should have kept her from the throne, but Isabella was a woman who defied the odds. Tough, determined, and iron-willed, Queen Isabella of Castile deftly maneuvered dynastic feuds and political rivalries. Together with her husband Ferdinand II of Aragon, she politically and religiously united Spain, routed the last Muslim stronghold in western Europe, and launched the age of exploration by backing Christopher Columbus. His voyages would lay the foundation for what would become the Spanish Empire. At the height of her power, one European observed, "This queen of Spain, called Isabella, has had no equal on this earth for 500 years".

A Kingdom Divided

When Isabella was born, Spain was not united. Instead, it was fractured into several small kingdoms. Her father, John II, ruled Castile. Meaning "land of castles," Castile had once been a small Christian power in northern Spain in the 10th century. As the centuries passed, it grew larger, gradually expanding south as Spain's Muslim rulers, the "Moors," were weakening.

Iberia's other Christian kingdoms were Aragon to the east, Navarre to the north, and Portugal to the west. These three other territories had their own royal families, who were deeply interrelated and constantly quarrelling over questions of succession. In negotiating these disputes, Isabella would prove to be as cunning as her older brother Henry was inept.

John II died in 1454, and Henry became king of Castile, ruling from the city of Segovia. He sent Isabella, her brother Alfonso, and their mother far away from court to Arévalo. Isabella was nevertheless given an education fit for a princess, and she was surrounded by a select group of ladies-in-waiting and tutors appointed by her father before he died. From them she received a substantial education of rhetoric, painting, philosophy, and history.

Struggling as king, Henry was unable to provide an heir. His childless first marriage was annulled, but not without having had his sexual prowess (or lack thereof) exposed before an ecclesiastic tribunal. His inability to plant the royal seed became a vexing political issue, giving him the moniker that would accompany him into history books: Henry the Impotent.

Henry married again in 1455, this time to the daughter of the king of Portugal. In 1462 she gave birth to a daughter, Joanna, but rumors about the girl's true paternity began to swirl. Some believed that Henry was not her biological father, and that the likeliest candidate was one of the king's—and possibly the queen's—favorites. Whether true or not, the courtly gossip only further undermined both Joanna's legitimacy and Henry's power.

Shortly before Joanna's birth, Henry summoned Isabella and Alfonso to Segovia to have more supervision and control over possible rivals to the throne. Their mother remained in Arévalo; Isabella would later describe how she was "inhumanely . . . torn from our mother's arms." She hated living at court and considered Henry's wife to be cruel and abusive.

Henry officially named his infant daughter Joanna heir to the throne of Castile. A powerful group of nobles used the rumors of Joanna's parentage to protest it. They backed Alfonso over Joanna as the true heir. In a risky move Isabella sided with her younger brother. Her daring paid off, for Henry relented; he named Alfonso his heir as long as Joanna were betrothed to him so that both would share the crown.

But Henry would later attempt to back out of this arrangement, and civil war erupted. The rebels crowned the young Alfonso king, but his "rule" never gained legitimacy. He died three years later, in 1468, and left Isabella as his heir. Some of the kingdom's barons were more than willing to rally around Isabella's claim.

Her more impetuous advisers urged Isabella to seize power without waiting for Henry to die. But the princess, though still a teenager, demonstrated keen political savvy. Presenting herself as a guarantor of the established order, she would quietly wait her turn while negotiating a stronger position for herself. Patience paid off; Henry signed an agreement in 1468 in which he recognized his half-sister as his legitimate successor. As part of the deal, she would not have to marry against her will, a distinct improvement over tradition. Isabella had the position she sought on her terms and would become queen after her older brother's death.

A Mate Selected

Isabella knew when to be patient and when to make a bold move, skills that served her well as she carefully navigated choosing a husband. Few detailed descriptions of the young Isabella exist, but chroniclers agree she had fair skin, blue eyes, and dark blonde hair, inherited from her English grandmother, Catherine of Lancaster. Isabella was sure to be courted, if not for her looks, then for her lands and her title.

As part of being Henry's heir, Isabella agreed to inform the king of any marriage proposals before a match was made. Marriage in the 15th century was a political tool, creating alliances between kingdoms. Henry and his backers wanted Isabella to marry King Afonso V of Portugal to unite the two kingdoms. Afonso was a widower and nearly 20 years older than Isabella. Rather than blindly submit to her brother's wishes, Isabella quietly decided to consider other suitors, ones more to her liking.

One of the leading candidates was Ferdinand, son of John II of Aragon. He was just a year younger than Isabella. In 1461 his father named Ferdinand heir to Aragon and the other lands under his control. Battle-tested Ferdinand appealed to Isabella. It would be smart to ally with Aragon, she decided, which was keen to unite with Castile to form a vast kingdom in Iberia. Throughout 1468 Isabella continued to be coy toward the Portuguese overtures, never outright rejecting marriage to its king, while she secretly entertained envoys from Aragon and discussed different marriage possibilities. By January 1469 she had made her choice, and it was Ferdinand.

Some historians have claimed that Isabella fell for Ferdinand's dashing reputation, that his youth and machismo tipped the scales. While this is a romantic story, it is more likely that Isabella was following her head and not her heart when she chose her mate. She suspected that once married to Afonso V, she would be forced to forfeit her power and become little more than a consort. With Ferdinand, she could craft a better deal to maintain her power even though she would be openly rebelling against her brother.

Marriage preparations were carried out in the utmost secrecy. According to their negotiations, Ferdinand could administer justice in Castile, but Isabella would retain power as queen over every other domain. Ferdinand could not even leave Castile without her permission. The engagement remained secret, but Isabella had to make a public demonstration of her loyalty to Aragon to seal the deal. She did so by leaving Ocaña, the town where Henry had placed her under the careful watch of his supporters. Without her brother's consent, she traveled to Madrigal de las Altas Torres, her birthplace, and from there to Valladolid in northern Castile, where the pair would marry.

In September 1469 Ferdinand set out from Aragon to join Isabella. Disguised as a servant, he rode in a small party of six to avoid attracting unwanted attention. Two days after Ferdinand's arrival, the couple met for the very first time. Four days later, Isabella and Ferdinand were wed. The marriage was duly consummated on the following day, in a nuptial chamber shared with a select group of witnesses. Official chroniclers presented their meeting as love at first sight, but both partners had a shared political interest in the marriage and practical reasons for making it work.

Many of Spain's noble families were closely related, which had led to power struggles in the past. In this case, Ferdinand and Isabella were second cousins. According to canon law, they required papal authorization to get married. Concerned by the consequences the marriage could have for the territories of Castile and Aragon, Pope Paul II refused to grant it.

When the wedding took place in October 1469, the archbishop of Toledo had presented a forged papal bull, of which the couple were no doubt aware. They repeatedly requested dispensation from Rome but did not obtain it until December. So, the woman who ended up receiving the title of "Catholic Queen," in fact married in defiance of church law. By the time she was pardoned, she had already given birth to her first child—a daughter, also named Isabella—in 1470.

Henry --was furious when he received news of the marriage. He rightly regarded Isabella as having infringed their pact and immediately decided to cancel her right of succession and return it to his daughter, Joanna. Isabella was not surprised by his reaction and might have even welcomed it. She never forgave Henry for cruelly separating her from her mother all those years ago; however, she did not directly challenge her brother for the throne while he lived. Instead, Isabella kept a cool head and bided her time.

One freezing December morning in 1474, news of Henry's death reached Isabella and Ferdinand. The following day Isabella solemnly proclaimed herself queen of Castile and demanded obedience from the main cities of the kingdom. Weeks later Joanna also proclaimed herself queen. She forged an alliance with Portugal by agreeing to marry her uncle (and Isabella's former suitor), King Afonso V.

Isabella would spend the first four years of her reign fighting a bloody civil war against Joanna and Portugal for the Castilian throne. It was during this conflict that her marriage to Ferdinand began to change. When they were engaged, Isabella held the political power, but war would place the couple on more even ground. With a common goal to unite them, they needed to trust in the other's loyalty and skills as each traveled separately to build armies and forge alliances. Over time the marriage strengthened and grew into one of mutual respect.

This partnership served them well, and by 1479 the two had defeated Joanna and Afonso. Isabella's grip on the throne of Castile was now secure. The victorious queen gave her niece a choice: be pledged to marry Isabella's one-year-old son John, or enter a convent in Portugal. Joanna chose the nunnery. When Ferdinand's father died later that year, Ferdinand became king of Aragon. The two kingdoms would be united, laying the groundwork for a united Spain in years to come.

Isabella's rise to power set the stage for a dramatic era in Spanish history, filled with turbulent highs and lows. She and Ferdinand completed the Reconquista, the centuries-long movement to end Muslim rule in Iberia. Granada, the last Muslim stronghold, fell in January 1492, and Iberia returned to full Christian control. Later that year in October, Isabella's decision to back Christopher Columbus unexpectedly paid off when he made landfall in the Caribbean. This expedition would lay the foundations for the Spanish Empire in the New World, making Spain a dominant player on the world stage.

Isabella's reign had its darker side too. The Spanish Inquisition began under her rule around 1480, persecuting Muslims and Jews who would not convert to Catholicism. In 1492 Isabella and Ferdinand ordered Spain's Jewish community to convert or be expelled. The Catholic Monarchs ventured down a dark path to unity through the terror and pain of others, a move that still casts dark shadows over Spanish history.

After 35 years of marriage, the union of Isabella and Ferdinand came to an end in 1504. Isabella died at the age of 52. Ferdinand mourned the loss, calling her "the best and most excellent wife a king ever had." Pious and devout, she asked in her will to be buried "in a low tomb with no structure other than a low slab on the floor," but her wishes were defied. Her tomb is suited to a queen of her stature, and Ferdinand would join her there 11 years later.

Source:

https://www.nationalgeographic.com/ **Full link:** https://rb.gy/ptcupr

Boudicca - Queen of Britain

Boudicca, also spelled Boadicea or Boudica, (died 60 or 61 CE), Boudica (also written as Boadicea) was a Celtic queen who led a revolt against Roman rule in ancient Britain in A.D. 60 or 61. As all of the existing information about her comes from Roman scholars, particularly Tacitus and Cassius Dio, little is known about her early life; it's believed she was born into an elite family in Camulodunum (now Colchester) around A.D. 30.

It is agreed that Boudica was of royal descent. Cassius Dio describes her as tall, with tawny hair hanging down to below her waist, a harsh voice and a piercing glare. He writes that she habitually wore a large golden necklace (perhaps a torc), a colorful tunic, and a thick cloak fastened by a brooch.

At the age of 18, Boudica married Prasutagas, king of the Iceni tribe of modern-day East Anglia. When the Romans conquered southern England in A.D. 43, most Celtic tribes were forced to submit, but the Romans let Prasutagas continue in power as a forced ally of the Empire. When he died without a male heir in A.D. 60, the Romans annexed his kingdom and confiscated his family's land and property. As a further humiliation, they publicly flogged Boudica and raped her two daughters. Tacitus recorded Boudicca's promise of vengeance after this last violation: "Nothing is safe from Roman pride and arrogance. They will deface the sacred and will deflower our virgins. Win the battle or perish, that is what I, a woman, will do".

Like other ancient Celtic women, Boudica had trained as a warrior, including fighting techniques and the use of weapons. With the Roman provincial governor Gaius Suetonius Paulinus leading a military campaign in Wales, Boudica led a rebellion of the Iceni and members of other tribes resentful of Roman rule. After defeating the Roman Ninth Legion, the queen's forces destroyed Camulodunum, then the captain of Roman Britain, and massacred its inhabitants. They went on to give similar treatment to London and Verulamium (modern St. Albans). By that time, Suetonius had returned from Wales and marshaled his army to confront the rebels. In the clash that followed–the exact battle site is unknown, but possibilities range from London to Northamptonshire – the Romans managed to defeat the Britons despite inferior numbers, and Boudica and her daughters apparently killed themselves by taking poison in order to avoid capture.

Tacitus also wrote about Boudicca: "Boudicca rode in a chariot with her daughters before her, and as she drew near to each tribe, she made it known that it was customary for the Britons to engage in warfare under the leadership of women. But, at this moment, she was not a woman descended from great ancestors avenging her kingdom and her wealth; rather she was one woman, from the common people, avenging the freedom she had lost, her body worn out with flogging, and the violated chastity of her daughters. The excessive desires of the Romans had advanced so much that they left nothing undefiled, not even the bodies of the old or those of young girls. Nonetheless the gods were at hand for just vengeance …. If the Britons considered the number of their men bearing arms and the reasons they were fighting, they must conquer on that field of battle or die. That was her purpose as a woman; as for the men, they could live on and be slaves (if they desired that)."

"At first, the legionaries stood motionless, keeping to the defile as a natural protection: then, when the closer advance of the enemy had enabled them to exhaust their missiles with certitude of aim, they dashed forward in a wedgelike formation. The auxiliaries charged in the same style; and the cavalry, with lances extended, broke a way through any parties of resolute men whom they encountered. The remainder took to flight, although escape was difficult, as the cordon of wagons had blocked the outlets. The troops gave no quarter even to the women: the baggage animals themselves had been speared and added to the pile of bodies. The glory won in the course of the day was remarkable, and equal to that of our older victories: for, by some accounts, little less than eighty thousand Britons fell, at a cost of some four hundred Romans killed and a not much greater number of wounded. Boudica ended her days by poison; while Poenius Postumus, camp-prefect of the second legion, informed of the exploits of the men of the fourteenth and twentieth, and conscious that he had cheated his own corps of a share in the honours and had violated the rules of the service by ignoring the orders of his commander, ran his sword through his body". Tacitus, Publius, Cornelius, The Annals, Book 14, Chapter 35

The Roman slaughter of women and animals was unusual, as they could have been sold for profit, and point to the mutual enmity between the two sides. According to Tacitus in his Annals, Boudica poisoned herself, though in the Agricola which was written almost twenty years before the Annals he mentions nothing of suicide and attributes the end of the revolt to socordia ("indolence"); Dio says she fell sick and died and then was given a lavish burial.

In all, Tacitus claimed, Boudica's forces had massacred some 70,000 Romans and pro-Roman Britons. Though her rebellion failed, and the Romans would continue to control Britain until A.D. 410, Boudica is celebrated today as a national heroine and an embodiment of the struggle for justice and independence.

Catus Decianus, who had fled to Gaul, was replaced by Gaius Julius Alpinus Classicianus. Suetonius conducted punitive operations, but criticism by Classicianus led to an investigation headed by Nero's freedman Polyclitus.

Fearing Suetonius's actions would provoke further rebellion, Nero replaced the governor with the more conciliatory Publius Petronius Turpilianus. The historian Gaius Suetonius Tranquillus tells us the crisis had almost persuaded Nero to abandon Britain. No historical records tell what had happened to Boudica's two daughters.

The location of Boudica's defeat is unknown. Some historians favour a site somewhere along the Roman road now known as Watling Street. Kevin K. Carroll suggests a site close to High Cross, Leicestershire, on the junction of Watling Street and the Fosse Way, which would have allowed the Legio II Augusta, based at Exeter, to rendezvous with the rest of Suetonius's forces, had they not failed to do so. Manduessedum (Mancetter), near the modern town of Atherstone in Warwickshire, has also been suggested, and according to legend "The Rampart" near Messing, Essex and Ambresbury Banks in Epping Forest. More recently, a discovery of Roman artefacts in Kings Norton close to Metchley Camp has suggested another possibility, one individual has suggested the Cuttle Mill area of Paulerspury in Northamptonshire, where fragments of Roman pottery from the 1st century have been found.

The location of Boudicca's grave, subject to much speculation, is unknown. Suggested locations include Birdlip in Gloucestershire, Stonehenge, Norfolk, London's Hampstead area, and somewhere under a train platform at King's Cross Station in London.

Sources:

https://www.academia.edu/ **Full link:** https://rb.gy/ecvzl1

https://www.britannica.com/biography/Boudicca

https://www.history.com/news/who-was-boudica

https://en.wikipedia.org/ **Full link:** https://rb.gy/dwt1eo

Empress Dowager Cixi of China (1835-1908)

The Concubine Who Launched Modern China by Jung Chang.

Is a vigorous defense of a ruthless ruler, and murderer, justified?

In her concluding judgment on the character and achievements of Cixi, the Qing dynasty's legendary empress dowager, Jung Chang observes: "In some four decades of absolute power, her political killings, whether just or unjust … were no more than a few dozen, many of them in response to plots to kill her."

Life at any court is a rough game: the combination of intimate emotions and absolute power generates a special form of cruelty in those who survive. A woman who began her adulthood as a 16-year-old grade-three imperial concubine in 1852, and rose to hold supreme power in the Manchu empire for the best part of 40 years, is likely to have a few unpleasant traits.

Nevertheless, a few dozen political murders – without counting the deaths further afield in suppressed rebellions and more distant wars – is not nothing. Her victims included the emperor Guangxu's son's favourite concubine, thrown down a well, and Guangxu himself, by then deposed by her, dispatched with arsenic on the eve of her own death to ensure that he made no comeback.

This approving biography advances a vigorous defense of a woman whom history has often demonized as a venal reactionary: one who murdered without a second thought to protect her own interests, who squandered the national treasury on her own pleasures and who set back reform in China to preserve herself. History often has trouble giving powerful women their due and correctives are in order, but Chang's admiration for her subject can sometimes seem a little unqualified: the empress dowager in these pages was an enlightened, even caring ruler who drove through a modernization programme. Had she lived just a little longer, China might have become a stable constitutional monarchy. As it is, Chinese citizens still cannot vote.

Where does the truth lie in Cixi's much told story? Her talents were highly regarded by many statesmen and officials who encountered or served her. She managed to steer the increasingly leaky ship of the Qing state through serious internal rebellions, foreign incursions and wars, trying to make the best of a weak position. Though protocol confined her to palace life and limited ritual journeys, she was eager to learn about foreign countries, customs and fashions and cultivated a shrewd strategic understanding of the world. That Cixi was a remarkable woman is not in doubt.

Born in 1835 into a family of Manchu government officials, the girl who would gain fame as the Empress Dowager Cixi showed no obvious signs of future greatness. This girl, both through good fortune and unyielding determination, would rise to power in China, becoming the Dowager Empress, ruling as the queen regent from 1861 until her death in 1908, one of the most turbulent periods in China's history. With her iron will and shrewd mind, she helped transform China from a medieval society to a modern power on the global stage.

Few concrete records remain of Cixi's life before age 16. She was Manchu, the ethnic minority in power since the 1600s, and her heritage kept her feet from being bound, a tradition of China's ethnic majority, the Han. Her family were most likely government employees. She probably could read, write, draw, and sew. Some historians say her father sought her advice and valued her opinion as highly as he would a son's.

She entered the Forbidden City as a concubine to the emperor Xianfeng. Although graded third rank, her standing in court improved in 1856 when she bore a son, a helpful move for a woman in China, even today.

Early in his reign, Xianfeng faced colossal problems on both domestic and foreign fronts. He came to power at age 18 in 1850, the same year that widespread famine caused the Taiping Rebellion, a massive peasant uprising in the southern provinces. This insurrection would continue unabated and leave a third of China under rebel control. Six years later, France and Britain invaded China, beginning the second Opium War and putting an enormous strain on the country's resources. This conflict also stirred up heated debates between pro- and anti-Western factions within China.

Cixi began to offer the emperor unwanted advice, inspiring in him the prophetic fear that she might interfere in state affairs after his death. In the face of all this turmoil, Emperor Xianfeng died in 1861, and Cixi's five-year-old son became the imperial heir, dubbed Emperor Tongzhi. Before his death, Xianfeng had selected eight men—princes and ministers from his inner circle—to form a Board of Regents and rule until his son came of age.

Cixi saw the emperor's death as a necessary moment to strike a blow to improve China. She thought the regents had poorly advised the emperor. Cixi, then known then as Concubine Yi, worked together with Zhen on a plan to launch a coup. She and Zhen were supported by two of Xianfeng's brothers, Prince Gong—an advocate of appeasing the West—and Prince Chun, who had married Yi's younger sister. The two women successfully overthrew the regents, imprisoning five of them, executing one, and ordering two to commit suicide. The dowager empresses would rule until the child emperor came of age. They took new names: Zhen became Ci'an ("kindly and serene"); and Yi took the name Cixi ("kindly and joyous") to mark the events.

Over the next five decades, China's fate was determined by Cixi. She managed to impose her authority in spite of the inferior position the strict court protocol gave to women: The widowed empress presided over meetings from behind a screen, as the ministers were not supposed to see her. She never entered the foremost section of the Forbidden City, which was reserved for the emperor. Instead she relied on loyal men to carry out her decisions, such as Prince Gong, who headed the Great Imperial Council. Since she governed behind the scenes, her achievements were attributed to others, while her opponents cast her as a crafty, bloodthirsty conspirator.

Manchu governors (who dominated the Han ethnic majority) were divided between those who opposed the Westerners and those who, like Cixi, wanted to modernize China to boost its economy in order to avoid total submission to the West, as well as Japan, which had become a serious threat to China.

In spite of the criticism, Cixi managed to bring peace to the country, put public finances on a sound footing, built a navy, and encouraged the country to open up to the world. With the help of the Westerners who commanded the army, the southern Taiping rebels were finally crushed.

Cixi advocated westernization—but not completely. For example, she took nearly 20 years to allow the complete construction of a railroad because she did not want to disturb ancestral tombs that lay near the proposed line. She did not want to promote textile factories because they took work away from Chinese women. She also knew there was much opposition to reform among the people, from commoners to civil servants to nobles, who detested so-called barbarian Western customs.

Since she could never sit on the throne herself, her continued power depended on the emperor being a child. In this, one might say, she had a lot of luck. Her own son died as a teenager in 1875. Some believed that power-hungry Cixi had poisoned her son to cling to power, but no proof for murder exists. Dark rumors circulated around Cixi, and not for the last time. Another child, her three-year-old nephew, succeeded as Emperor Guangxu. Cixi promptly adopted him, though, bizarrely, she instructed him to address her as "my royal father". It was not a warm relationship. The death of the former empress Zhen, which some would add to Cixi's account, left Cixi in sole charge and her reluctance to hand over the reins on the boy's maturity was palpable.

She embarked on a second wave of modernization, introducing electricity and coal mining. She started a war with France to oppose its territorial ambitions on the border between China and Vietnam, which ended in a stalemate.

She reluctantly "retired" in 1889 when the young emperor came of age, and devoted herself to building a pleasure ground on the outskirts of Beijing.

It was not the last of her. Guangxu was suspicious of everything Western. His failure to comprehend the modern world later led him to abandon China's naval program, resulting in a crushing defeat to Japan in 1894.

She came out of retirement to help with the trauma of a losing the war against Japan. After which she retained an active role in state affairs, a position that left her well placed for her next coup.

In 1898, Guangxu, who had good reason to dislike his "royal father" launched a radical reform programme under the guidance of two former imperial scholars, Kang Youwei and Liang Qichao, and against the resistance of the more conservative elements at court. Kang – portrayed here one-dimensionally as a scheming upstart – persuaded the emperor that Cixi was an obstacle that had to be neutralized. Kang involved the emperor in a plot to assassinate Cixi, but their plans were discovered as Cixi moved first. by September 1898, she had deposed and imprisoned Guangxu and taken the reins again herself. Those reformers who did not escape were executed. Also executed were two entirely innocent men, whose trials Cixi had stopped to prevent the emperor's role in the plot to assassinate her becoming public.

The last few years of Cixi's career were no less dramatic and mirror the contradictions in her record. Her biggest mistake was to encourage the disastrous Boxer rebellion, a violent anti-foreign and anti-Christian movement that culminated in a bloody siege of the foreign legations in Beijing. That ended in a punitive foreign rescue and huge indemnities to the countries concerned. China, and Cixi, paid a heavy price for what she later admitted was a mistake. She herself had to flee the capital, pausing only to order the killing of Guangxu's favourite concubine. When she returned to the capital she was chastened, and set about making friends with the ladies of the Legation quarter, the wives of the resident diplomats, in a belated effort to restore her reputation in the world. She launched her own reform programme within two years, using the exiled Kang Youwei's blueprint.

In January 1902 Cixi announced a series of reforms that shook up all aspects of Chinese life. Marriages between Han and Manchu partners were legalized. Foot-binding, a custom long practiced on Han girls, was banned. Freedom of the press was expanded. In 1906 Cixi announced that China would be transformed into a constitutional monarchy with elections.

She died in 1908, having poisoned Guangxu with arsenic the day before, thus creating what was to be the final vacancy on the Dragon throne. It was filled by the child Pu Yi, the last emperor: in 1911 the empire fell and Pu Yi abdicated the following year. China began the long, bloody and unfinished process of trying to become a modern republican state. In 1927, under the KMT (nationalist) government, Cixi's tomb was dynamited by robbers, her jewels and her teeth stolen and her body left exposed.

Although most of Cixi's previous biographers have demonized her, others have been more measured. This is a spirited, if partisan contribution. Her role in crushing the reforms of 1898 and her support of the Boxer rebellion remain her most controversial actions. Did the reformers' plot against her excuse the dismantling of reforms that she was to borrow wholesale just a few years later?

Jung Chang praises these as proof of Cixi's progressive character; others have judged them as too little too late, grudging concessions that failed to save the rule of the Manchu – outnumbered 100 to one by their Chinese subjects.

The times that Cixi dominated were critical to the shaping of modern China, a country that resembles the Qing autocracy in many ways, though without the empire's relatively free press and anticipated suffrage. The top echelons of Chinese politics remain as male-dominated and vicious as ever, and Cixi remains as gripping a subject.

Sources:

https://www.theguardian.com/ **Full link:** https://rb.gy/sdjlvu

https://www.nationalgeographic.com/ **Full Link:** https://rb.gy/pbz87g

Theodora (497-548) - Empress of Byzantium

Theodora reigned as empress of the Byzantine Empire alongside her husband, Emperor Justinian I, from 527 CE until her death in 548 CE. Rising from a humble background and overcoming the prejudices of her somewhat disreputable early career as an actress, Theodora would marry Justinian (r. 527-565 CE) in 525 CE and they would rule together in a golden period of Byzantine history. Portrayed by contemporary writers as scheming, unprincipled, and immoral, the Empress, nevertheless, was also seen as a valuable support to the Emperor, and her direct involvement in state affairs made her one of the most powerful women ever seen in Byzantium.

Early Life

Theodora was born in c. 497 CE, the daughter of a bear-keeper called Akakios who worked for the Hippodrome of Constantinople. The 6th-century CE Byzantine historian Procopius of Caesarea states in his Secret History (Anekdota) that Theodora earned her living, like her mother before her, as an actress, which meant performing in the Hippodrome as an acrobat, dancer, and stripper. Theodora was said to have had one particularly lurid routine involving geese. By implication, considering the common association of the two professions at the time, she was also a courtesan. Procopius would have us believe an especially popular and lustful one, at that.

Procopius' Secret History, is, though, regarded by many as an outrageous gossip piece with a few facts thrown in for authenticity. The writer's attitude to both Justinian and Theodora is plainly that they were the worst thing ever to happen to the Byzantine Empire (in contrast to the official works he wrote under Justinian's patronage which are suitably laudatory of the emperor's achievements in war and architecture especially). Procopius also had it in for Antonina, the wife of Belisarius (Justinian's most talented general), and she is portrayed as constantly scheming with Theodora to create damaging palace intrigues. It is perhaps important to consider, too, that our knowledge of Theodora only comes from male authors and a woman performing any other role than the traditionally submissive one in Byzantine society was bound to be, at best, disapproved of and, at worst, outright demonized.

Before she married Justinian, the nephew of Emperor Justin (r. 518-527 CE), in 525 CE, Theodora left the sands of the Hippodrome to travel to North Africa as the mistress of a medium-level civil servant. After the relationship broke up, she made her way back home via Alexandria where she may have converted to Christianity.

The marriage between such a lowly figure as Theodora and a future emperor was an odd rags-to-riches one, but there was a tradition in the Byzantine court for emperors to marry the winners of beauty contests organized for that purpose. The entrants to such contests could come from lower classes and from far away provinces so such mismatches were not unheard of. The lowly status of Theodora was not ignored by everyone, and one particularly passionate opponent was Empress Lupicina Euphemia, indeed, her death seems to have removed the foremost obstacle to the marriage. Justin I even went so far as to amend the laws (senators, which

Justinian was, could not marry actresses) in order to permit the marriage and to legitimize Theodora's illegitimate daughter. Procopius also claims there was an illegitimate son, too, but no other sources substantiate this.

The Empress, 20 years younger than her husband, is described by Procopius as being short but attractive, a stickler for court ceremony, and a lover of luxury. Theodora was crowned as empress in the same coronation ceremony as her husband on 1st April 527 CE. Justinian had insisted his wife be crowned as his equal and not as his consort. The pair also matched each other in intelligence, ambition, and energy, and with their lavish coronation in the Hagia Sophia, they seemed to herald a new era for the Byzantine Empire and its people.

The Nika Revolt

Theodora's active role in Byzantine politics and the staunch support she gave her husband are best revealed by the incident of the Nika Revolt of 11th-19th January 532 CE. This was an infamous riot caused by factions of the supporters in the Hippodrome of Constantinople. The real causes for complaint were Justinian's tax hikes (to pay for his incessant military campaigns) and his general autocracy, but the riot was sparked by the emperor's refusal to pardon Blue and Green supporters for a recent outburst of violence in the Hippodrome. The troublemakers joined forces for once, and using the ominous chant "Conquer!" (Nika), which they usually screamed at the particular charioteer they were supporting in a race, they organized themselves into an effective force.

The trouble began with Justinian's appearance in the Hippodrome on the occasion of the opening races of the games. The crowd turned on their emperor, the races were abandoned and the rioters spilt out of the Hippodrome to rampage through the city. They left an impressive trail of destruction wherever they marched, burning down the Church of Hagia

Sophia, the Church of Saint Irene, the baths of Zeuxippus, the Chalke gate, and a good portion of the Augustaion forum including, significantly, the Senate House. The starting point of all this destruction, the Hippodrome, escaped with only minor damage. The riot had become a full-scale rebellion and Hypatios, the general and nephew of Anastasius I (r. 491-518 CE), was crowned in the Hippodrome as the new emperor by the rioters.

Justinian was not to be so easily pushed from his throne, although it is Theodora who is credited with persuading the Emperor not to flee the mob but stand firm and fight. Her words at that crucial moment were recorded by Procopius as follows:

"I do not care whether or not it is proper for a woman to give brave counsel to frightened men; but in moments of extreme danger, conscience is the only guide. Every man who is born into the light of day must sooner or later die; and how can an Emperor ever allow himself to become a fugitive? If you, my Lord, wish to save your skin, you will have no difficulty in doing so. We are rich, there is the sea, there too are our ships. But consider first whether, when you reach safety, you will not regret that you did not choose death in preference. As for me, I stand by the ancient saying: royalty makes the best shroud. (quoted in Brownworth, 79-80)."

The imperial cause was greatly helped by the gifted generals Belisarius and Mundus, who ruthlessly quashed the revolt by slaughtering 30,000 of the perpetrators inside the Hippodrome. Hypatios, who had not actually wished to be crowned by the rioters, was executed nonetheless. No games were held in the Hippodrome for several years after the crisis, but one happy consequence of the whole destructive episode was the required rebuilding programme which resulted in the construction of the present version of the Hagia Sophia church.

Attitude to the Church

Theodora's religious policies seem to have been entirely her own, they were certainly not those of her husband, the leader of the Byzantine church and protector of orthodoxy. The Empress favoured Monophysitism, that is the belief that Jesus Christ had only one, divine nature (physis), which went against the orthodox view that he had two natures - one human and one divine. Nor were her views merely theoretical ponderings, for Theodora acted upon them and protected and housed priests and monks who adhered to monophysite beliefs, even using the Great Palace of Constantinople to do so. Indeed, the Empress is credited with the promotion of, and ultimately achieving the adoption of, Monophysitism in Nubia around 540 CE.

Political Intrigues

Theodora's political manoeuvres are blamed for the downfall of the chief minister John of Cappadocia, although he was none too popular with the Byzantine people either because he was seen as the instigator of the oppressive tax reforms which had caused the Nika Revolt. Procopius, too, paints the finance minister as a paradigm of corruption and debauchery. John was dismissed after the revolt as one of the demands of the rioters but he later made a political comeback. It was then that Theodora was said to have conspired against him out of personal hatred. John was thus banished from court in 541 CE.

Other victims of the Empress' machinations were Pope Silverius (deposed in 537 CE) and possibly the Gothic queen Amalasuntha, who was assassinated, but real details and hard evidence are lacking. Belisarius was another who found himself in Theodora's bad books. He might have been a great general, perhaps Byzantium's greatest, but his success only aroused the suspicions of the empress, who may well have coloured her husband's dealings with his foremost commander, which resulted in a lack of material support in the field of battle when needed.

Worse was to follow for Belisarius when the devastating bubonic plague struck the empire in the spring of 542 CE. Justinian himself was infected; he survived, but while he was gravely ill, Theodora ruled alone. Seeing that if her husband died, and with no heir to play regent for, her position would be untenable, the Empress moved quickly against the general she regarded as her greatest rival for the throne. Belisarius was too popular a figure to simply imprison or murder but he could be cut down a peg or two, and so Theodora ordered he be relieved of his command and his property be confiscated. Fortunately for the general, when Justinian recovered the following year and with the Moors and Goths baying at the frontiers of the empire, he was restored to his former position.

Procopius also states that the Empress was not slow to place her own friends and associates in positions of power at court. Besides these darker tales of personal vendettas and cronyism, Theodora was noted for her influence on Justinian's social reforms and her charitable work, sponsoring the foundation of many institutions for the poor such as orphanages, hospitals, and (perhaps significantly given her former profession) a home for former prostitutes seeking to reenter respectable society.

Death

Theodora died in 548 CE, aged just 51 or 52, probably of cancer. Justinian had no heir but, perhaps significantly, he never remarried. Theodora's daughter from before her marriage to Justinian had three sons and all of these became prominent figures in the Byzantine court. Justinian, after a period a deep mourning, would rule for another 17 years but he never seemed quite so focused or as brilliant as when he had had Theodora by his side.

Procopius might have stolen the accolades for most-lasting and colourful literary portrait of the Empress but, in the visual arts, there is a formidable rival to how Theodora is remembered in history. This most celebrated of depictions is in the church of San Vitale in Ravenna, Italy. The glittering wall mosaic shows the Empress in one panel while another shows Justinian and the archbishop of Ravenna, Maximian (r. 546-556 CE). Theodora, like her husband, is portrayed with a large halo. She is also wearing a great deal of jewellery with necklaces, earrings, and a fabulous gem-studded crown, and a Tyrian purple robe. She presents to the church a jewelled gold chalice and is surrounded by officials and her extensive entourage of court ladies.

Source: https://www.ancient.eu/Empress_Theodora/

Diana, Princess of Wales (1961–1997)

The late Diana, Princess of Wales was born The Honorable Diana Frances Spencer on 1st July 1961 in Norfolk. She received the style Lady Diana Spencer in 1975, when her father inherited his Earldom.

Lady Diana Spencer married The Prince of Wales at St Paul's Cathedral in London on 29th July 1981.

During her marriage the Princess undertook a wide range of royal duties. Family was very important to the Princess, who had two sons: Prince William and Prince Henry (Harry). After her divorce from The Prince of Wales, the Princess continued to be regarded as a member of the Royal Family.

Diana, Princess of Wales, died on Sunday, 31st August 1997, following a car crash in Paris.

There was widespread public mourning at the death of this popular figure, culminating with her funeral at Westminster Abbey on Saturday, 6th September 1997.

Even after her death, the Princess's work lives on in the form of commemorative charities and projects set up to help those in need.

Diana, Princess of Wales, formerly Lady Diana Frances Spencer, was born on 1st July 1961 at Park House near Sandringham, Norfolk. She was the youngest daughter of the then Viscount and Viscountess Althorp, now the late (8th) Earl Spencer and the late Hon. Mrs. Shand-Kydd, daughter of the 4th Baron Fermoy. Until her father inherited the Earldom, she was styled The Honorable Diana Spencer.

Viscount Althorp was Equerry to George VI from 1950 to 1952, and to The Queen from 1952 to 1954. Lady Diana's parents, who had married in 1954, separated in 1967 and the marriage was dissolved in 1969. Earl Spencer later married Raine, Countess of Dartmouth in 1976.

Together with her two elder sisters Sarah (born 1955), Jane (born 1957) and her brother Charles (born 1964), Diana continued to live with her father at Park House, Sandringham, until the death of her grandfather, the 7th Earl Spencer. In 1975, the family moved to the Spencer seat at Althorp (a stately house dating from 1508) in Northamptonshire, in the English Midlands.

Lady Diana was educated first at a preparatory school, Riddlesworth Hall at Diss, Norfolk, and then in 1974 went as a boarder to West Heath, near Sevenoaks, Kent. At school she showed a particular talent for music (as an accomplished pianist), dancing and domestic science, and gained the school's award for the girl giving maximum help to the school and her schoolfellows.

She left West Heath in 1977 and went to finishing school at the Institute Alpin Videmanette in Rougemont, Switzerland, which she left after the Easter term of 1978. The following year she moved to a flat in Coleherne Court, London. For a while she looked after the child of an American couple, and she worked as a kindergarten teacher at the Young England School in Pimlico.

On 24th February 1981 it was officially announced that Lady Diana was to marry The Prince of Wales. As neighbors at Sandringham until 1975, their families had known each other for many years, and Lady Diana and The Prince had met again when he was invited to a weekend at Althorp in November 1977.

They were married at St Paul's Cathedral in London on 29th July 1981, in a ceremony which drew a global television and radio audience estimated at around 1,000 million people, and hundreds of thousands of people lining the route from Buckingham Palace to the Cathedral. The wedding reception was at Buckingham Palace.

The marriage was solemnized by the Archbishop of Canterbury Dr. Runcie, together with the Dean of St. Paul's; clergy from other denominations read prayers. Music included the hymns "Christ is made the sure foundation", "I vow to thee my country", the anthem "I was glad" (by Sir Hubert Parry), a specially composed anthem "Let the people praise thee" by Professor Mathias, and Handel's "Let the bright seraphim" performed by Dame Kiri te Kanawa. The lesson was read by the Speaker of the House of Commons, Mr. George Thomas (the late Lord Tonypandy).

The Princess was the first Englishwoman to marry an heir to the throne for 300 years (when Anne Hyde married the future James II from whom The Princess was descended). The bride wore a silk taffeta dress with a 25-foot train designed by the Emanuels, her veil was held in place by the Spencer family diamond tiara, and she carried a bouquet of gardenias, lilies-of-the-valley, white freesia, golden roses, white orchids and stephanotis. She was attended by five bridesmaids, including Princess Margaret's daughter Lady Sarah Armstrong-Jones (now Lady Sarah Chatto). Prince Andrew (now The Duke of York) and Prince Edward (now The Earl of Wessex) were The Prince of Wales's Supporters (a Royal custom instead of a Best Man).

The Prince and Princess of Wales spent part of their honeymoon at the Mountbatten family home at Broadlands, Hampshire, before flying to Gibraltar to join the Royal Yacht HMY BRITANNIA for a 12-day cruise through the Mediterranean to Egypt. They finished their honeymoon with a stay at Balmoral.

The Prince and Princess made their principal home at Highgrove House near Tetbury, Gloucestershire, with an apartment in Kensington Palace as their London home.

They had two sons. Prince William Arthur Philip Louis was born on 21st June 1982 and Prince Henry (Harry) Charles Albert David on 15th September 1984, both at St Mary's Hospital, Paddington, in London. The Princess had 17 godchildren.

In December 1992 it was announced that The Prince and Princess of Wales had agreed to separate. The Princess based her household and her office at Kensington Palace, while The Prince was based at St. James's Palace and continued to live at Highgrove.

In November 1995 The Princess gave a television interview during which she spoke of her unhappiness in her personal life and the pressures of her public role. The Prince and Princess were divorced on 28th August 1996.

The Prince and Princess continued to share equal responsibility for the upbringing of their children. The Princess continued to be regarded as a member of the Royal Family.

The Queen, The Prince and The Princess of Wales agreed that the Princess was to be known after the divorce as Diana, Princess of Wales, without the style of 'Her Royal Highness' (as The Princess was given the style 'HRH' on marriage she would therefore be expected to give it up on divorce). The Princess continued to live at Kensington Palace, with her office based there.

After her marriage, The Princess of Wales quickly became involved in the official duties of the Royal Family.

Her first tour with The Prince of Wales was a three-day visit to Wales in October 1981. In 1983 she accompanied the Prince on a tour of Australia and New Zealand, and they took the infant Prince William with them. Prince William, with Prince Harry, again joined The Prince and Princess of Wales at the end of their tour to Italy in 1985.

Other official overseas visits undertaken with the Prince included Australia (for the bicentenary celebrations in 1988), Brazil, India, Canada, Nigeria, Cameroon, Indonesia, Spain, Italy, France, Portugal and Japan (for the enthronement of Emperor Akihito). Their last joint overseas visit was to South Korea in 1992.

The Princess's first official visit overseas on her own was in September 1982, when she represented The Queen at the State funeral of Princess Grace of Monaco. The Princess's first solo overseas tour was in February 1984, when she travelled to Norway to attend a performance of Carmen by the London City Ballet, of which she was Patron. The Princess subsequently visited many countries including Germany, the United States, Pakistan, Switzerland, Hungary, Egypt, Belgium, France, South Africa, Zimbabwe and Nepal.

Although the Princess was renowned for her style and was closely associated with the fashion world, patronizing and raising the profile of younger British designers, she was best known for her charitable work.

During her marriage, the Princess was president or patron of over 100 charities. The Princess did much to publicize work on behalf of homeless and also disabled people, children and people with HIV/Aids.

In December 1993, the Princess announced that she would be reducing the extent of her public life in order to combine "a meaningful public role with a more private life".

After her separation from The Prince of Wales, the Princess continued to appear with the Royal Family on major national occasions, such as the commemorations of the 50th anniversary of VE (Victory in Europe) and VJ (Victory over Japan) Days in 1995.

Following her divorce, the Princess resigned most of her charity and other patronages, and relinquished all her Service appointments with military units. The Princess remained as patron of Centrepoint (homeless charity), English National Ballet, Leprosy Mission and National Aids Trust, and as President of the Hospital for Sick Children, Great Ormond Street and of the Royal Marsden Hospital.

In June 1997, the Princess attended receptions in London and New York as previews of the sale of a number of dresses and suits worn by her on official engagements, with the proceeds going to charity.

The Princess spent her 36th and last birthday on 1st July 1997 attending the Tate Gallery's 100th anniversary celebrations. Her last official engagement in Britain was on 21st July, when she visited Northwick Park Hospital, London (children's accident and emergency unit).

In the year before her death, the Princess was an active campaigner for a ban on the manufacture and use of land mines. In January 1997, she visited Angola as part of her campaign. in June, the Princess spoke at the landmines conference at the Royal Geographical Society in London, and this was followed by a visit to Washington DC in the United States on 17th/18th June to promote the American Red Cross landmines campaign (separately, she also met Mother Teresa in the Bronx, New York). The Princess's last public engagements were during her visit to Bosnia from 7th to 10th August, when she visited landmine projects in Travnic, Sarajevo and Zenezica.

It was in recognition of her charity work that representatives of the charities with which she worked during her life were invited to walk behind her coffin with her family from St. James's Palace to Westminster Abbey on the day of her funeral.

Death

The tragic death of Diana, Princess of Wales occurred on Sunday 31st August 1997 following a car accident in Paris, France.

The vehicle in which The Princess was travelling was involved in a high-speed accident in the Place de l'Alma underpass in central Paris shortly before midnight on Saturday 30th August.

The Princess was taken to the La Pitie Salpetriere Hospital, where she underwent two hours of emergency surgery before being declared dead at 0300 BST. The Princess's companion, Mr. Dodi Fayed, and the driver of the vehicle died in the accident, whilst a bodyguard was seriously injured.

The Princess's body was subsequently repatriated to the United Kingdom in the evening of Sunday 31st August by a BAe 146 aircraft of the Royal Squadron. The Prince of Wales and the Princess's elder sisters, Lady Sarah McCorquodale and Lady Jane Fellowes, accompanied The Princess's coffin on its return journey.

Upon arrival at RAF Northolt, the coffin, draped with a Royal Standard, was removed from the aircraft and transferred to a waiting hearse by a bearer party from The Queen's Colour Squadron of the RAF. The Prime Minister was among those in the reception party.

From RAF Northolt the coffin was taken to a private mortuary in London, so that the necessary legal formalities could be completed. Shortly after midnight, it was moved to the Chapel Royal in St James's Palace, where it lay privately until Friday 5th September, when it was taken to Kensington Palace for the last night before the funeral on Saturday 6th September, in Westminster Abbey. The Princess's family and friends visited the Chapel to pay their respects.

Following the funeral service, the coffin then was taken by road to the family estate at Althorp for a private internment. The Princess was buried in sanctified ground on an island in the center of an ornamental lake.

Source:

https://www.royal.uk/diana-princess-wales

Margaret Thatcher (1925–2013) – The Iron Lady

The first female prime minister of Britain, Margaret Thatcher was a controversial figurehead of conservative ideology during her time in office.

Who Was Margaret Thatcher?

Margaret Thatcher became Britain's Conservative Party leader and in 1979 was elected prime minister, the first woman to hold the position. During her three terms, she cut social welfare programs, reduced trade union power and privatized certain industries. Thatcher resigned in 1991 due to unpopular policy and power struggles in her party. She died on April 8th, 2013, at age 87.

Early Life

Thatcher was born as Margaret Hilda Roberts on October 13th, 1925, in Grantham, England. Nicknamed the "Iron Lady", Thatcher served as the prime minister of England from 1979 to 1990. The daughter of a local businessman, she was educated at a local grammar school, Grantham Girls' High School. Her family operated a grocery store and they all lived in an apartment above the store. In her early years, Thatcher was introduced to conservative politics by her father, who was a member of the town's council.

A good student, Thatcher was accepted to Oxford University, where she studied chemistry at Somerville College. One of her instructors was Dorothy Hodgkin, a Nobel Prize-winning scientist. Politically active in her youth, Thatcher served as president of the Conservative Association at the university. She earned a degree in chemistry in 1947 and went on to work as a research chemist in Colchester. Later, she worked as a research chemist in Dartford.

Early Foray into Politics

Two years after graduating from college, Thatcher made her first bid for public office. She ran as the conservative candidate for a Dartford parliamentary seat in the 1950 elections. Thatcher knew from the start that it would be nearly impossible to win the position away from the liberal Labour Party. Still, she earned the respect of her political party peers with her speeches. Defeated, Thatcher remained undaunted, trying again the following year, but once more her efforts were unsuccessful. Two months after her loss, she married Denis Thatcher.

In 1952, Thatcher put politics aside for a time to study law. She and her husband welcomed twins Carol and Mark the next year. After completing her training, Thatcher qualified as a barrister, a type of lawyer, in 1953. But she didn't stay away from the political arena for too long. Thatcher won a seat in the House of Commons in 1959, representing Finchley.

Clearly a woman on the rise, Thatcher was appointed parliamentary undersecretary for pensions and national insurance in 1961. When the Labour Party assumed control of the government, she became a member of what is called the Shadow Cabinet, a group of political leaders who would hold Cabinet-level posts if their party was in power.

When Conservatives returned to office in June 1970, Thatcher was appointed secretary of state for education and science, and dubbed "Thatcher, milk snatcher," after her abolition of the universal free school milk scheme. She found her position frustrating, not because of all the bad press around her actions, but because she had difficulty getting Prime Minister Edward Heath to listen to her ideas. Seemingly disenchanted on the future of women in politics, Thatcher was quoted as saying, "I don't think there will be a woman prime minister in my lifetime," during a 1973 television appearance.

Thatcher soon proved herself wrong. While the Conservative Party lost power in 1974, Thatcher became a dominant force in her political party. She was elected leader of the Conservative Party in 1975, beating out Heath for the position. With this victory, Thatcher became the first woman to serve as the opposition leader in the House of Commons. England was in a time of economic and political turmoil, with the government nearly bankrupt, employment on the rise and conflicts with labor unions. This instability helped return Conservatives to power in 1979. As party leader, Thatcher made history in May 1979, when she was appointed Britain's first female prime minister.

Conservative Leadership

As prime minister, Thatcher battled the country's recession by initially raising interest rates to control inflation. She was best known for her destruction of Britain's traditional industries through her attacks on labor organizations such as the miner's union, and for the massive privatization of social housing and public transport. One of her staunchest allies was U.S. President Ronald Reagan, a fellow conservative. The two shared similar right-wing, pro-corporate political philosophies.

Thatcher faced a military challenge during her first term. In April 1982, Argentina invaded the Falkland Islands. This British territory had long been a source of conflict between the two nations, as the islands are located off the coast of Argentina. Taking swift action, Thatcher sent British troops to the territory to retake the islands in what became known as the Falklands War. Argentina surrendered in June 1982.

In her second term, from 1983 to 1987, Thatcher handled a number of conflicts and crises, the most jarring of which may have been the assassination attempt against her in 1984. In a plot by the Irish Republic Army, she was meant to be killed by a bomb planted at the Conservative Conference in Brighton in October. Undaunted and unharmed, Thatcher insisted that the conference continue, and gave a speech the following day.

As for foreign policy, Thatcher met with Mikhail Gorbachev, the Soviet leader, in 1984. That same year, she signed an agreement with the Chinese government regarding the future of Hong Kong. Publicly, Thatcher voiced her support for Reagan's air raids on Libya in 1986 and allowed U.S. forces to use British bases to help carry out the attack.

Resignation

Returning for a third term in 1987, Thatcher sought to implement a standard educational curriculum across the nation and make changes to the country's socialized medical system. However, she lost a lot of support due to her efforts to implement a fixed rate local tax—labeled a poll tax by many since she sought to disenfranchise those who did not pay it. Hugely unpopular, this policy led to public protests and caused dissension within her party.

Thatcher initially pressed on for party leadership in 1990, but eventually yielded to pressure from party members and announced her intentions to resign on November 22nd, 1990. In a statement, she said, "Having consulted widely among colleagues, I have concluded that the unity of the Party and the prospects of victory in a General Election would be better served if I stood down to enable Cabinet colleagues to enter the ballot for the leadership. I should like to thank all those in Cabinet and outside who have given me such dedicated support." On November 28th, 1990, Thatcher departed from 10 Downing Street, the prime minister's official residence, for the last time.

Life After Politics

Not long after leaving office, Thatcher was appointed to the House of Lords, as Baroness Thatcher of Kesteven, in 1992. She wrote about her experiences as a world leader and a pioneering woman in the field of politics in two books: The Downing Street Years (1993) and The Path to Power (1995). In 2002, she published the book Statecraft, in which she offered her views on international politics.

Around this time, Thatcher suffered a series of small strokes. She then suffered a great personal loss in 2003, when her husband of more than 50 years, Denis, died. The following year, Thatcher had to say goodbye to an old friend and ally, Ronald Reagan. In fragile health, Thatcher gave a eulogy at his funeral via video link, praising Reagan as a man who "sought to mend America's wounded spirit, to restore the strength of the free world, and to free the slaves of communism."

In 2005, Thatcher celebrated her 80th birthday. A huge event was held in her honor and was attended by Queen Elizabeth II, Tony Blair and nearly 600 other friends, family members and former colleagues. Two years later, a sculpture of the strong conservative leader was unveiled in the House of Commons.

Final Years and Legacy

Thatcher's health made headlines in 2010, when she missed a celebration at 10 Downing Street, held in honor of her 85th birthday by David Cameron. Later, in November 2010, Thatcher spent two weeks in the hospital for a condition that was later revealed to cause painful muscle inflammation. In 2011, she sat out such a number of major events, including the wedding of

Prince William in April, and the unveiling of the Ronald Reagan sculpture in London in July. Additionally, in July 2011, Thatcher's office in the House of Lords was permanently closed. The closure has been seen by some to mark the end of her public life.

Battling memory problems in her later years due to her strokes, Thatcher retreated from the spotlight, living in near seclusion at her home in London's Belgravia neighborhood.

Thatcher died on April 8th, 2013, at the age of 87. She was survived by her two children, daughter Carol and son Sir Mark. Thatcher's policies and actions continue to be debated by detractors and supporters alike, illustrating the indelible impression that she has left on Britain and nations worldwide.

Source:

https://www.biography.com/political-figure/margaret-thatcher

Indira Gandhi (1917-1984) – 1st Female Indian Prime Minister

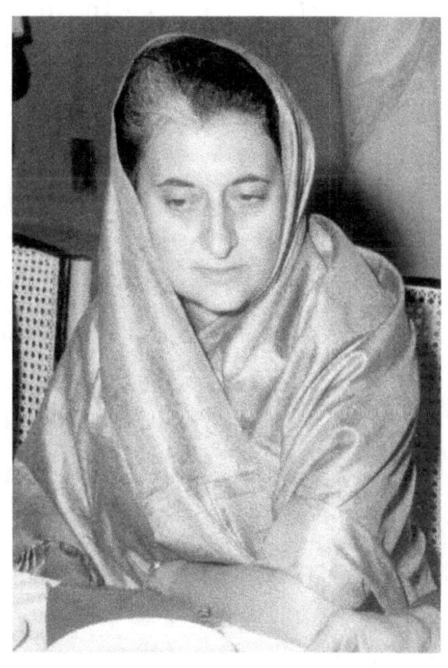

The only daughter of Prime Minister Jawaharlal Nehru, Indira Gandhi was destined for politics. First appointed prime minister in 1966, she garnered widespread public support for agricultural improvements that led to India's self-sufficiency in food grain production as well as for her success in the Pakistan war, which resulted in the creation of Bangladesh in 1971. After serving three terms, Gandhi was voted out of office for her increasingly authoritarian policies, including a 21-month state of emergency in which Indians' constitutional rights were restricted. In 1980, however, she was reelected to a fourth term. Following a deadly confrontation at the Sikh's holiest temple in Punjab four years later, Gandhi was assassinated by two of her bodyguards on October 31st, 1984, ushering her son Rajiv into power and igniting extensive anti-Sikh riots.

Early Life and Family

Born on November 19th, 1917, in Allahabad, India, Indira Priyadarshini Gandhi was the sole child of Kamala and Jawaharlal Nehru. As a member of the Indian National Congress, Nehru had been influenced by party leader

Mahatma Gandhi, and dedicated himself to India's fight for independence. The struggle resulted in years of imprisonment for Jawaharlal and a lonely childhood for Indira, who attended a Swiss boarding school for a few years, and later studied history at Somerville College, Oxford. Her mother passed away in 1936 of tuberculosis.

In March 1942, despite the disapproval of her family, Indira married Feroze Gandhi, a Parsi lawyer (unrelated to Mahatma Gandhi), and the couple soon had two sons: Rajiv and Sanjay.

Political Career and Accomplishments

In 1947, Nehru became the newly independent nation's first prime minister, and Gandhi agreed to go to New Delhi to serve as his hostess, welcoming diplomats and world leaders at home and traveling with her father throughout India and abroad. She was elected to the prominent 21-member working committee of the Congress Party in 1955 and, four years later, was named its president. Upon Nehru's death in 1964, Lal Bahadur Shastri became the new prime minister, and Indira took on the role of Minister of Information and Broadcasting. But Shastri's leadership was short-lived; just two years later he abruptly died and Indira was appointed by Congress Party leaders to be prime minister.

Within a few years Gandhi gained enormous popularity for introducing successful programs that transformed India into a country self-sufficient in food grains—an achievement known as the Green Revolution.

In 1971, she threw her support behind the Bengali movement to separate East from West Pakistan, providing refuge for the ten million Pakistani civilians who fled to India in order to escape the marauding Pakistan army and eventually offering troops and arms. India's decisive victory over Pakistan in December led to the creation of Bangladesh, for which Gandhi was posthumously awarded Bangladesh's highest state honor 40 years later.

Following the 1972 national elections, Gandhi was accused of misconduct by her political opponent and, in 1975, was convicted of electoral corruption by the High Court of Allahabad and prohibited from running in another election for six years. Instead of resigning as expected, she responded by declaring a state of emergency on June 25th, whereby citizens' civil liberties were suspended, the press was acutely censored and the majority of her opposition was detained without trial. Throughout what became referred to as the "Reign of Terror," thousands of dissidents were imprisoned without due process.

Anticipating that her former popularity would assure her re-election, Gandhi finally eased the emergency restrictions and called for the next general election in March 1977. Riled by their limited liberties, however, the people overwhelmingly voted in favor of the Janata Party and Morarji Desai assumed the role of prime minister.

Within the next few years, democracy was restored, but the Janata Party had little success in resolving the nation's severe poverty crisis. In 1980, Gandhi campaigned under a new party—Congress (I)—and was elected into her fourth term as prime minister.

Assassination

In 1984, the holy Golden Temple in Amritsar, Punjab, was taken over by Sikh extremists seeking an autonomous state. In response, Gandhi sent Indian troops to regain the temple by force. In the barrage of gunfire that ensued, hundreds of Sikhs were killed, igniting an uprising within the Sikh community.

On October 31st, 1984, Indira Gandhi was assassinated outside her home by two of her trusted bodyguards, seeking retribution for the events at the temple.

1- Her life involved politics from a young age

Almost from the moment she was born in 1917, Indira Nehru's life was steeped in politics. Her father, Jawaharlal Nehru, was a leader in the fight for India's independence from British rule, so it was natural for Indira to become a supporter of this struggle.

One tactic of India's nationalist movement was to reject foreign — particularly British — products. At a young age, Indira witnessed a bonfire of foreign goods. Later, the 5-year-old chose to burn her own beloved doll because the toy had been made in England.

When she was 12, Indira played an even bigger role in India's struggle for self-determination by leading children in the Vanar Sena (the name means Monkey Brigade; it was inspired by the monkey army that aided Lord Rama in the epic Ramayana). The group grew to include 60,000 young revolutionaries who addressed envelopes, made flags, conveyed messages and put up notices about demonstrations. It was a risky undertaking, but Indira was happy to be participating in the independence movement.

2- Her marriage wasn't widely supported

Indira's father was a close associate of Mahatma Gandhi. However, the fact that Indira ended up with the same last name as the iconic Indian leader wasn't due to a connection with the Mahatma; instead, Indira became Indira Gandhi following her marriage to Feroze Gandhi (who wasn't related to the Mahatma). And despite the fact that Indira and Feroze were in love, theirs was a wedding that few people in India supported.

Feroze, a fellow participant in the struggle for independence, was Parsi, while Indira was Hindu, and at the time mixed marriages were unusual. It was also out-of-the-norm not to have an arranged marriage. In fact, there was such a public outcry against the match that Mahatma Gandhi had to offer a public statement of support, which included the request: "I invite the writers of abusive letters to shed your wrath and bless the forthcoming marriage."

Indira and Feroze wed in 1942. Unfortunately, though the pair had two sons together, the marriage was not a great success. Feroze had extramarital liaisons, while much of Indira's time was spent with her father after he became India's prime minister in 1947. The marriage ended with Feroze's death in 1960.

3- A refugee crisis put pressure on her

In 1971, Indira faced a crisis when troops from West Pakistan went into Bengali East Pakistan to crush its independence movement. She spoke out against the horrific violence on March 31st, but harsh treatment continued and millions of refugees began to stream into neighboring India.

Taking care of these refugees stretched India's resources; tensions also mounted because India offered support to independence fighters. Making the situation even more complicated were geopolitical considerations — President Richard Nixon wanted the United States to stand by Pakistan and China was arming Pakistan, while India had signed a "treaty of peace, friendship and cooperation" with the Soviet Union. The situation didn't improve when Indira visited the United States in November — Oval Office recordings from the time reveal that Nixon told Henry Kissinger the prime minister was an "old witch."

War began when Pakistan's air force bombed Indian bases on December 3rd; Indira recognized the independence of Bangladesh (formerly East Pakistan) on December 6th. On December 9th, Nixon directed a U.S. fleet to head for Indian waters — but then Pakistan surrendered on December 16th.

The war's conclusion was a triumph for India and Indira (and, of course, for Bangladesh). After the conflict had ended, Indira declared in an interview, "I am not a person to be pressured — by anybody or any nation".

4- Millions were sterilized when she declared a state of emergency

In June 1975, Indira was found guilty of electoral malpractice. When rivals began advocating for her removal as prime minister, she opted to declare a state of emergency. Emergency rule would be a dark moment for India's democracy, with opponents imprisoned and press freedoms limited. Perhaps most shockingly, millions of people were sterilized — some against their will — during this period.

At the time, population control was seen as necessary in order for India to prosper (Indira's favored son and confidant, Sanjay, became particularly focused on reducing the birth rate). During the Emergency, the government directed its energies toward sterilization, with a focus on the simpler procedure of vasectomies. To encourage men to undergo the operation, incentives such as cooking oil and cash were offered.

Then government workers began to be required to meet sterilization quotas to get paid. Reports came out that vasectomies had been performed on boys, and that men were being arrested, then sent to be sterilized. Some began sleeping in fields so as to avoid sterilization teams. According to a 1977 article in TIME magazine, between April 1976 and January 1977, 7.8 million were sterilized (the initial target had been 4.3 million).

At the beginning of 1977, Indira called for elections, ending her Emergency rule. She'd expected to win this vote, but the fear and worries brought on by the sterilization policy contributed to her defeat at the polls, and she was kicked out of office.

5- She was close with Margaret Thatcher

As a female leader in the 20ᵗʰ century, Indira Gandhi was a member of a very small club. Yet she had one friend who could understand what her life was like: The Iron Lady herself, Britain's Margaret Thatcher.

Indira and Thatcher first met in 1976. They got on well, despite the fact that Indira was engaged in her undemocratic Emergency rule at the time. And when Indira was temporarily out of power after her electoral defeat in 1977, Thatcher didn't abandon her. The two continued to have a good rapport after Indira returned to power in 1980.

When Thatcher came close to being killed by an IRA bomb in October 1984, Indira was sympathetic. Following Indira's own assassination a few weeks later, Thatcher ignored death threats to attend the funeral. The note of condolence that she sent to Rajiv stated: "I cannot describe to you my feelings at the news of the loss of your mother, except to say that it was like losing a member of my own family. Our many talks together had a closeness and mutual understanding which will always remain with me. She was not just a great statesman but a warm and caring person".

6- Her son succeeded her after her death

One significant factor that buoyed Indira's political career was her heritage. As the daughter of India's first prime minister, the Congress Party was happy to put her in a position of leadership, then later selected her to become prime minister.

After Indira's 1984 assassination, her son Rajiv succeeded her as prime minister. In 1991, he was also assassinated, but the Nehru-Gandhi clan still wasn't done with politics: though Rajiv's widow, Sonia, initially declined the Congress Party's request to step into a leadership role, she eventually became its president. By the 2014 election, Rajiv and Sonia's son Rahul had joined the

Congress Party as well; however, the party went on to experience a big loss at the polls. At a press conference, Rahul admitted, "The Congress has done pretty badly, there is a lot for us to think about. As vice president of the party I hold myself responsible."

Yet not all Gandhis fared poorly in the 2014 election — as members of the victorious Bharatiya Janata Party, Maneka Gandhi and her son Varun are now in power, with Maneka serving as minister of women and child development (though considering her acrimonious relationship with Maneka, this development likely wouldn't thrill Indira). And despite their poor showing in 2014, the Congress Party refused to accept Sonia and Rahul's resignations. It seems that various members of Indira's family will continue to play a role in Indian politics for the foreseeable future.

Sources:

https://www.history.com/topics/india/indira-gandhi
https://www.biography.com/ **Full link:** https://rb.gy/20x8zg

Sirimavo Bandaranaike (1916-2000) - Prime Minister of Sri Lanka

Sirimavo Bandaranaike, in full Sirimavo Ratwatte Dias Bandaranaike, also called Sirimavo R.D. Bandaranaike, (born April 17th, 1916, Ratnapura, Ceylon (now Sri Lanka)—died October 10th, 2000, Colombo, Sri Lanka).

Born into an aristocratic Kandyan family, Bandaranaike was educated in Catholic, English-medium schools, but remained a Buddhist and spoke Sinhala as well as English.

After completing her schooling at age 19, Sirima Ratwatte became involved in social work, distributing food and medicine to jungle villages, organizing clinics and helping create rural industry to improve the living standards of village women. She became the treasurer of the Social Service League, serving in that capacity until 1940. Over the next six years, she lived with her parents while they arranged her marriage. After rejecting two suitors – a relative, and the son of the first family of Ceylon – Ratwatte's parents were contacted by a matchmaker who proposed a union with Solomon West Ridgeway Dias (S.W.R.D.) Bandaranaike, an Oxford-educated lawyer-turned-politician, who was at the time Minister of Local Administration in the State Council of Ceylon.

Playing hostess to her husband S. W. R. D. Bandaranaike, who was involved in politics and later became Prime Minister, she gained his trust as an informal advisor. Following her husband's assassination in 1959, Bandaranaike was induced by his Sri Lanka Freedom Party (SLFP) to become the party's leader. The SLFP won a decisive victory at the general election in July 1960, and she became prime minister.

Social Work (1940–1959)

In 1941 Bandaranaike joined the Lanka Mahila Samiti (Lankan Women's Association), the country's largest women's voluntary organization. She participated in many of the social projects initiated by the Mahila Samiti for the empowerment of rural women and disaster relief. One of her first projects was an agricultural programme to meet food production shortages. Her first office, as secretary of the organization, involved meeting with farming experts to develop new methods for producing yields of rice crops.

She was also a member of the All Ceylon Buddhist Women's Association, the Cancer Society, the Ceylon National Association for the Prevention of Tuberculosis, and the Nurses Welfare Association.

Bandaranaike often accompanied S.W.R.D. on official trips, both locally and abroad. She and her husband were both present after the psychiatric hospital in Angoda was bombed by the Japanese during the Easter Sunday Raid in 1942, killing many. As Ceylon moved toward self-governing status in 1947, S.W.R.D. became more active in the nationalist movement. He ran for – and was elected to – the House of Representatives from the Attanagalla Electoral District. He was appointed Minister of Health and served as Leader of the House, but became increasingly frustrated with the inner workings and policies of the United National Party. Though he did not encourage Bandaranaike to engage on political topics and was dismissive of her in front of colleagues, S.W.R.D. came to respect her judgment. In 1951, she persuaded him to resign from the United National Party and establish the Sri Lanka Freedom Party (Freedom Party, aka SLFP). Bandaranaike campaigned in

S.W.R.D.'s Attanagalla constituency during the 1952 parliamentary election, while he travelled around the country to garner support. Though the Freedom Party won only nine seats during that election, S.W.R.D. was elected to Parliament and became Leader of the Opposition.

When fresh elections were called in 1956 by Prime Minister Sir John Kotelawala, S.W.R.D. sensed an opportunity and formed the Mahajana Eksath Peramuna (MEP), a broad four-party coalition, to contest the 1956 elections. Bandaranaike once again campaigned for her husband in Attanagalla, in her home town of Balangoda, and in Ratnapura for the Freedom Party. The Mahajana Eksath Peramuna won a landslide victory and S.W.R.D. became the Prime Minister.

Bandaranaike was at home in Rosmead Place on the morning of 25th September 1959, when S.W.R.D. Bandaranaike was shot multiple times by a Buddhist monk, disgruntled over what he believed to be lack of support for traditional medicine. Bandaranaike accompanied her husband to hospital where he succumbed to his wounds the following day. In the political chaos that followed under the caretaker government of Wijeyananda Dahanayake, many cabinet ministers were removed, and some were arrested and tried for the assassination. The Mahajana Eksath Peramuna coalition collapsed without S.W.R.D.'s influence, and elections were called for March 1960 to fill the seat for the Attanagalla constituency. Bandaranaike reluctantly agreed to run as an independent candidate, but before the election could be held, Parliament was dissolved, and she decided not to contest the seat. When the election was held in March 1960, the United National Party won a four-seat majority over the Sri Lanka Freedom Party. Dudley Senanayake, the new Prime Minister, was defeated within a month in a vote of confidence and a second general election was called for July 1960.

Political Career

In May 1960, Bandaranaike was unanimously elected party president by the executive committee of the Freedom Party, although at the time she was still undecided about running in the July election. Disavowing former party ties with Communists and Trotskyists, by early June she was campaigning with promises to carry forward the policies of her husband – in particular, establishing a republic, enacting a law to establish Sinhala as the official language of the country, and recognizing the predominance of Buddhism, though tolerating the estate Tamils use of their own language and Hindu faith. Though there had been Tamil populations in the country for centuries, the majority of the estate Tamils had been brought to Ceylon from India by the British colonizers as plantation workers. Many Ceylonese viewed them as temporary immigrants, even though they had lived for generations in Ceylon. With Ceylon's independence, the Citizenship Act of 1948 excluded these Indian Tamils from citizenship, making them stateless. S.W.R.D.'s policy toward the stateless Tamils had been moderate, granting some citizenship and allowing productive workers to remain. His successor, Dudley Senanayake, was the first to recommend compulsory repatriation for the population. Bandaranaike toured the country and made emotional speeches, frequently bursting into tears as she pledged herself to continue her late husband's policies. Her actions earned her the title "The Weeping Widow" from her opponents.

First Female Prime Minister (1960–1965)

On 21st July 1960, following a landslide victory for the Freedom Party, Bandaranaike was sworn in as the first female prime minister in the world, as well as Minister of Defence and External Affairs. As she was not an elected member of parliament at the time, but leader of the party holding the majority in parliament, the constitution required her to become a member of Parliament within three months if she was to continue holding office as Prime Minister. To make a place for her, Manameldura Piyadasa de Zoysa resigned his seat in the Senate.

To further her husband's policy of nationalizing key sectors of the economy, Bandaranaike established a corporation with public-private shareholders, taking control of seven newspapers. She nationalized banking, foreign trade, and insurance, as well as the petroleum industry. In taking over the Bank of Ceylon and establishing branches of the newly created People's Bank, Bandaranaike aimed to provide services to communities with no previous banking facilities, spurring local business development. In December 1960, Bandaranaike nationalized all the parochial schools that were receiving state funding. In doing so she curtailed the influence of the Catholic minority, who tended to be members of the economic and political elite, and extended the influence of Buddhist groups. In January 1961, Bandaranaike implemented a law-making Sinhala the official language, replacing English. This action caused wide discontent among the more than two million Tamil-speakers. Urged on by members of the Federal Party, a campaign of civil disobedience began in the provinces with Tamil majorities. Bandaranaike's response was to declare a state of emergency and send in troops to restore peace. Beginning in 1961, trade unions began a series of strikes in protest to high inflation and taxes. One such strike immobilized the transport system, motivating Bandaranaike to nationalize the transport board.

At home, difficulties were mounting. Despite her success abroad, Bandaranaike was criticized for her ties with China and lack of economic development policies. Tensions were still high over the government's apparent favouritism of Sinhala-speaking Ceylonese Buddhists. The import-export imbalance, compounded by inflation, was impacting the buying power of middle- and lower-class citizens. In the mid-year by-election, although Bandaranaike held a majority, the United National Party made gains, indicating that her support was slipping. Lack of support for austerity measures, specifically the inability to import adequate rice – the main dietary staple – caused the resignation of Minister Felix Dias Bandaranaike. Other cabinet ministers were reassigned in an attempt to stem the drift toward Soviet trade partnerships, which had gained ground after the creation of the Ceylon Petroleum Corporation. The Petroleum Corporation had been launched in 1961 to bypass the monopolistic pricing imposed on Middle Eastern oil imports, allowing Ceylon to import oil from the United Arab Republic and the Soviet Union. Some of the storage facilities of western oil operatives were co-opted with a compensation agreement, but continuing disputes over non-payment resulted in suspension of foreign aid from the United States in February 1963. In reaction to the suspension of aid, the Parliament passed the Ceylon Petroleum Corporation Amendment Act nationalizing all distribution, import-export, sales and supply of most oil products in the country, from January 1964.

With that said, by 1964 a deepening economic crisis and the SLFP's coalition with the Marxist Lanka Sama Samaja Party ("Ceylon Socialist Party") had eroded popular support for her government, which was resoundingly defeated in the general election of 1965.

Leader of the Opposition (1965–1970)

In the 1965 elections, Bandaranaike won a seat in the House of Representatives from the Attanagalla Electoral District. With her party gaining 41 seats, she became the Leader of the Opposition, the first woman ever to hold the post. Dudley Senanayake was sworn in as Prime Minister on 25th March 1965. Soon after, Bandaranaike's position as a member of parliament was challenged, when allegations were made that she had accepted a bribe, in the form of a car, while in office. A committee was appointed to investigate and she was later cleared of the charge. During her five-year term in the opposition, she maintained her alliance with leftist parties. Of the seven by-elections held between November 1966 and April 1967, six were won by the opposition under Bandaranaike's leadership. Continued inflation, trade imbalance, unemployment, and the failure of expected foreign aid to materialize led to widespread discontent. This was further fuelled by austerity measures, which reduced the weekly rice stipend. By 1969, Bandaranaike was actively campaigning to return to power.

Second Term (1970–1977)

Bandaranaike regained power after the United Front coalition between the Communist Party, the Lanka Sama Samaja Party and her own Freedom Party won the 1970 elections with a large majority in May 1970. By July, she had convened a Constitutional Assembly to replace the British-drafted constitution with one drafted by the Ceylonese. She introduced policies requiring that permanent secretaries in the government ministries have expertise in their division.

Facing budget deficits of $195 million – caused by rising energy and food-importation costs and declining revenue from coconut, rubber and tea exports – Bandaranaike attempted to centralize the economy and implement price controls. Pressed by the leftist members of her coalition to nationalize the foreign banks of British, Indian and Pakistani origin, she realized that doing so would impact the need for credit. As she had in her previous regime, she tried to balance the flow of foreign assistance from both capitalist and communist partners. In September 1970, Bandaranaike attended the third Non-Aligned Conference in Lusaka, Zambia. That month, she also travelled to Paris and London to discuss international trade. Ordering representatives of The Asia Foundation and the Peace Corps to leave the country, Bandaranaike began re-evaluating trade agreements and proposals that had been negotiated by her predecessor. She announced that her government would not recognize

Israel, until the country peacefully settled its problem with its Arab neighbours. She officially granted recognition to East Germany, North Korea, North Vietnam, and the National Liberation Front of South Vietnam. Bandaranaike opposed the development of an Anglo-US communications center in the Indian Ocean, maintaining that the area should be a "neutral, nuclear-free zone". In December, the Business Undertaking Acquisition Act was passed, allowing the state to nationalize any business with more than 100 employees. Ostensibly, the move aimed to reduce foreign control of key tea and rubber production, but it stunted both domestic and foreign investment in industry and development.

In May 1972, Ceylon was replaced by the Republic of Sri Lanka after a new Constitution was ratified. Though the country remained within the Commonwealth of Nations, Queen Elizabeth II was no longer recognized as its sovereign. Under its terms, the Senate, suspended since 1971, was officially abolished and the new unicameral National State Assembly was created, combining the powers of the executive, judicial and legislative branches in one authority. The constitution recognized the supremacy of Buddhism, though it guaranteed equal protection to Buddhism, Christianity, Hinduism, and Islam. It failed to provide a charter of inalienable rights, recognized Sinhala as the only official language, and contained no "elements of federalism". The new constitution also extended Bandaranaike's term by two years, resetting the mandated five-year term of the Prime Minister to the coincide with the creation of the republic. These limits caused concern for various sectors of the population, specifically those who were uneasy about authoritarian rule, and the Tamil-speaking population. by the end of the year, a second wave of revolt was anticipated. Widespread unemployment fuelled the public's growing disillusionment with the government, in spite of land redistribution programmes enacted to establish farming cooperatives and limit the size of privately held lands.

Fissures appeared in the United Front coalition, largely resulting from the Lanka Sama Samaja Party's continued influence on trade unions and threats of strike actions throughout 1974 and 1975. When newly confiscated estates were placed under the Ministry of Agriculture and Lands, controlled by the Lanka Sama Samaja Party, fears that they would unionize plantation workers led Bandaranaike to oust them from the government coalition.

With all that said, while reducing inequalities of wealth, Bandaranaike's socialist policies had once again caused economic stagnation, and her government's support of Buddhism and the Sinhalese language had helped alienate the country's large Tamil minority. The failure to deal with ethnic rivalries and economic distress led, in the election of July 1977, to the SLFP's retaining only 8 of the 168 seats in the National Assembly, and Bandaranaike was replaced as prime minister.

In 1980 the Sri Lanka parliament stripped Bandaranaike of her political rights and barred her from political office, but in 1986 Pres. J.R. Jayawardene granted her a pardon that restored her rights. She ran unsuccessfully as the SLFP's candidate for president in 1988, and after regaining a seat in parliament in 1989 she became the leader of the opposition.

Leader of the Opposition (1989–1994)

On 6th February 1989, while campaigning for the Freedom Party in the 1989 general election, Bandaranaike survived a bombing attack. Though she was unscathed, one of her aides suffered leg injuries. In the final results on the 19th, the Freedom Party was defeated by the United National Party under Ranasinghe Premadasa, but gained 67 seats, sufficient for Bandaranaike to take up the post of Leader of the Opposition for a second term.

Bandaranaike's children, in the meantime, had become major political figures within the SLFP. Her son, Anura P.S.D. Bandaranaike, was first elected to parliament in 1977 and had become the leader of the SLFP's right-wing faction by 1984. He was frustrated in his bid to become the party's leader, however, by his sister Chandrika Bandaranaike Kumaratunga, who held left-wing views and was favoured by their mother for the leadership. In response, Anura defected from the SLFP and joined the rival United National Party (UNP) in 1993.

In 1990, when the 13-month ceasefire was broken by the Tamil Tigers, after other militias surrendered their weapons, the government decided to break off negotiations with the Tigers and employ a military solution. Anura supported the move, but his mother, Bandaranaike, spoke against the plan. When emergency powers were assumed by the president, she demanded that the state of emergency be lifted, accusing the government of human rights abuses. During her tenure as opposition leader, she supported the impeachment of Premadasa in 1991, which was led by senior United National Party members such as Lalith Athulathmudali and Gamini Dissanayake. The impeachment failed.

Bandaranaike's daughter Chandrika Kumaratunga, who had been living in self-imposed exile in London since 1988, when her husband had been assassinated, returned to Sri Lanka and rejoined the Freedom Party in 1991. In the same year, Bandaranaike, who was increasingly impaired by arthritis, suffered a stroke.

Third Term (1994–2000)

In the presidential election that took place in November 1994, Kumaratunga's main political rival, Gamini Dissanayake, was assassinated two weeks before the election. His widow, Srima Dissanayake, was chosen as the United National Party's presidential candidate. Kumaratunga's lead was predicted to be around a million votes even before the assassination: she won the election by a wide margin. Becoming the first female President of Sri Lanka, Kumaratunga appointed her mother as prime minister, which under the terms of the 1978 constitution meant Bandaranaike was responsible for defence and foreign affairs. Though the office of prime minister had become mainly a ceremonial post, Bandaranaike's influence in the Freedom Party remained strong. While they agreed on policy, Kumaratunga and Bandaranaike differed on leadership style. By 2000, Kumaratunga wanted a younger prime minister, and Bandaranaike, citing health reasons, stepped down in August 2000.

Death and Legacy

Bandaranaike died on 10th October 2000 of a heart attack at Kadawatha. Bandaranaike's remains lay in state in the parliament, and her funeral subsequently took place at Horagolla where she was interred in the mausoleum, Horagolla Bandaranaike Samadhi, originally built for her husband.

At a time in history when the idea of a woman leading a country was almost unthinkable to the public, Bandaranaike helped raise the global perception of women's capabilities. In addition to her own contributions to Sri Lanka, her children became involved in the development of the country. All three children held nationally prominent positions; in addition to Anura and Chandrika's roles in government, Bandaranaike's daughter Sunetra worked as her political secretary in the 1970s and later became a philanthropist. The Bandaranaike marriage helped break down social barriers in Sri Lanka over the years, through the Socialist policies they enacted.

During her three terms in office, Bandaranaike led the country away from its colonial past and into its political independence as a republic. Implementing socialist policies during the Cold War, she attempted to nationalize key sectors of the economy and undertake land reforms to benefit the native population, desiring to end the political favouritism enjoyed by the Western-educated elites.

As one of the founders of the Non-Aligned Movement, Bandaranaike brought Sri Lanka to prominence among the nations which sought to remain neutral to the influence of the superpowers.

Sources:

https://en.wikipedia.org/wiki/Sirimavo_Bandaranaike
https://www.britannica.com/ **Full link:** https://rb.gy/vcanhw

THANK YOU!